Learning Compassion

Learning Compassion

Conflict Resolution through Education and Therapy

Jacquelyn Ane Rinaldi
Clifford Mayes

ROWMAN & LITTLEFIELD
Lanham • Boulder • New York • London

Published by Rowman & Littlefield
An imprint of The Rowman & Littlefield Publishing Group, Inc.
4501 Forbes Boulevard, Suite 200, Lanham, Maryland 20706
www.rowman.com
86-90 Paul Street, London EC2A 4NE, United Kingdom

Copyright © 2023 by Jacquelyn Ane Rinaldi and Clifford Mayes

All rights reserved. No part of this book may be reproduced in any form or by any electronic or mechanical means, including information storage and retrieval systems, without written permission from the publisher, except by a reviewer who may quote passages in a review.

British Library Cataloguing in Publication Information Available

Library of Congress Cataloging-in-Publication Data

Names: Rinaldi, Jacquelyn Ane, 1972– author. | Mayes, Clifford, author.
Title: Learning compassion : conflict resolution through education and therapy / Jacquelyn Ane Rinaldi, Clifford Mayes.
Description: Lanham : Rowman & Littlefield Publishing Group, 2022. | Includes bibliographical references and index. | Summary: "Learning Compassion marshals depth psychology and Buddhism, primarily, as a means of promoting less aggressive, more productive approaches to tension in human affairs"— Provided by publisher.
Identifiers: LCCN 2022034029 (print) | LCCN 2022034030 (ebook) | ISBN 9781475869187 (cloth) | ISBN 9781475869194 (paperback) | ISBN 9781475869200 (epub)
Subjects: LCSH: Compassion—Religious aspects—Buddhism.
Classification: LCC BQ4360 .R56 2022 (print) | LCC BQ4360 (ebook) | DDC 294.3/5677—dc23/eng/20220808
LC record available at https://lccn.loc.gov/2022034029
LC ebook record available at https://lccn.loc.gov/2022034030

JR: To Ward, my beloved, I love the adventure we share. To Mom and Dad, thank you for always believing in me.

CM: To my wife, Evelyn; my daughter, Lizzy; my son, Josh, and my grandchildren, Noa, Eitan, and Noey-Noey. I learn so much from each of you, my teachers in the educative act that is my life.

Contents

Introduction	The Horizons of Compassion	ix
Chapter 1	The Theory of War and the Case for Peace	1
Chapter 2	Educating Psyche in Compassion	41
Chapter 3	Psychological Wholeness	79
Conclusion:	The Limits of War and Peace in Education and Therapy	103
	Bibliography	107
	Index	115

Introduction

The Horizons of Compassion

Compassion is often misunderstood. To live with compassion does not mean to give up one's own well-being or to jeopardize the well-being of her family in order to serve the needs of others. Compassion means one must first take care of herself before she is able to tend to another. True compassion can exist only within the framework of a well-balanced psyche—even-mindedness. It takes healthy self-esteem to realize one's own limits and set clear and direct boundaries to protect those limits. Compassion means being deeply human and at the same time honoring one's self and others.

Compassion, like muscle memory and rote memorization, is cultivated through practice. The current research from the field of neuroscience interprets compassion as a learned behavior as well as delineating that meditation is one of the most powerful tools for cultivating compassion and other balanced neurological states of being.

If we cultivated meditation, as we do reading and writing, as a part of the educational process for children from toddlers, through higher education, would that, in time change, what seems to be our addiction to the Ares archetype—war? At the very least, some students will see more compassionately, relate to life with more empathy, meet challenges with more optimism, and live with a greater sense of well-being and resilience. At best most of our children will grow up with these life-affirming qualities that have power beyond measure to heighten the collective to live in a more peaceful state of consciousness.

This book discusses the relationship between compassion and peace with a special emphasis on the role that education can play in promoting a state of affairs in which, as humanity becomes more compassionate, peace becomes more possible. It will take generations . . . but let us begin.

Different Voices on Violence

Many scholars of the subject say that peace is not possible in this world; in fact, James Hillman, one of the leading Jungians of the twentieth century, argued that war is an essential part of human nature. Sigmund Freud believed there are instincts for hatred and destruction in the human being. C. G. Jung also believed that aggression forms an essential part of the archetypal structure of psychospiritual functioning. From a Jungian perspective a person is both warlike and peaceful; conflict is cooperation's shadow side. Alfred Adler describes the primary issue with the propensity toward aggression and war as being the insatiable drive of human beings to attain power over others. He believed that the striving for power as a primary purpose is a false ideal that must be replaced by an ideal of social interest.

This study explores the topic of compassion through the lenses of Buddhism and depth psychology. The archetypes of war—including Ares, Mars, Indra, and Thor—suggest the permanence of the energies that these symbols represent. Hillman says, "War belongs to our souls as an archetypal truth of the cosmos" (2005, p. 214). He continues, "Wars will go on; they will not cease and they will not change. The dead will fall as ever. At least we can imagine and therefore understand—not all of it, but enough to step away from delusions of hope and love and peace and reason" (2005, p. 217).

In 1932, Albert Einstein wrote a letter, in service of the League of Nations, to Freud (1964/1981, p. 199) inquiring about the psychological aspects of war, "Is there any way of delivering mankind from the menace of war?" Freud responded that human beings do have a tendency toward war. "It is a general principle, then, that conflicts of interest between men are settled by the use of violence. This is true of the whole animal kingdom, from which men have no business to exclude themselves" (1964/1981, p. 204).

In the letter, Freud averred that humanity is not capable of ridding itself of aggression, not because it is not possible but because humanity will not adequately feed that which fosters cooperation. He declared that "the attempt to replace actual force by the force of ideas seems at present to be doomed to failure. . . . But one thing we can say: whatever fosters the growth of civilization works at the same time against war" (1964/1981, p. 208/215). Freud believes that what fosters civilization, community, and unity has the potential to create different solutions other than war. While he expresses little probability for seeing a world without war, there is a thread of hope in his thoughts, nevertheless.

Jung explained, along with Freud, that every human being has in him or her the potential to be warlike and at the same time cooperative. Jung believed that the perfect union is the balance of the two polar energies, warlike and cooperative. One cannot be fully good or completely evil. It is not in escaping one's aggressive nature but in balancing one's cooperative nature that one begins to see other possibilities beyond war as a solution for dealing with conflict.

His Holiness the 14th Dalai Lama asserts, on the other hand, that human beings are capable of learning and thereby choosing compassion. He writes, "In fact, secular techniques for compassion training are already in use and their effectiveness has even been scientifically demonstrated. . . . The more we train our abilities, the stronger they become" (2011, p. 56).

Similarly, the historian of religion Karen Armstrong observes, "Those who have persistently trained themselves in the art of compassion manifest new capacities in the human heart and mind; they discover that when they reach out consistently towards others, they are able to live with the suffering that inevitably comes their way with serenity, kindness, and creativity" (2010, pp. 22–23). Learned compassion creates the opportunity for a peaceful resolution to conflict instead of resorting to violence as a response.

This study explores the discrepancy between the common notion that war will always be present and the relationship of compassion to a more peaceful existence. It is our position that teachers such as the Dalai Lama, Thich Nhat Hanh, Jack Kornfield, Richard Davidson, and Karen Armstrong provide a substantial argument, documented by both science and experience, for an alternative point of view to the belief that frequent warfare is simply the human condition.

Anger and aggression are a part of human nature, to be sure. With that we agree. But the expression of war is an infantile way of dealing with that anger and aggression. Compassion is inversely connected to aggression; as compassion increases, war decreases. It is not an all-or-nothing affair. What we are aiming for is a steady diminution in warfare, always aiming at the ideal of completely eliminating it, but understanding (as in approaching the asymptotic limit in calculus) we may always fall a little short of the ultimate formula.

Depth psychology in conjunction with the psychology of Buddhism makes a contribution to the way compassion is understood, developed, and practiced. In depth psychology one begins by looking directly at one's complexes. The deeper the complexes, the more debris stands in the way of seeing the underlying unity of the human psyche that makes compassion possible. Jung names this unity, or oneness, the "Unus Mundus," and describes it as, "the original, non-differentiated unity of the world or of Being . . ." (1955–1956/1970a, *CW 14*, para. 660). People's complexes create ineffective thinking and dysfunctional feelings, along with feelings of frustration, fear, and other perplexing emotions. These emotions not only make it very challenging to see with compassionate eyes; they make it much more likely to see with conflicted and confused eyes that make actual conflict more probable.

This is not to say that once people become conscious of these complexes they are free from frustration and fear. But if a person investigates her inner barriers to see the Self, she develops tools for dealing with frustration, anger, and fear so that she is able to move more effectively through these challenges as they arise. It is through the individuation process that one begins to engage the archetype of the Self, which Jung defines as the archetype of unity and wholeness. Anthony Storr explains that "the self, of which the mandala is a symbol, is the archetype of unity and totality" (Jung, 1983, p. 20). Unity, totality, wholeness: different words for describing an inner state of acceptance, completion, being at rest, and peace—the very opposite of the conditions necessary for the instantiation and pursuit of war.

Marie-Louise von Franz describes the process of evolving toward unity and wholeness: "The first stage shows the process of the inner unification of the personality in the individuation process. The second stage, however, refers to a special process that always accompanies individuation in the single person; namely, the development of relatedness to certain fellow human beings and to mankind as a whole, a relatedness that proceeds not from the ego but from a transcendental inner center, the Self" (1978/1980, p. 174). It is the archetype of the Self which fosters compassion. As von Franz illuminates it, this process comes from a place of wholeness where merely cognitive understanding becomes meaningful. She writes, "The moment at which the insight is 'ripe' depends on the archetype of the Self, of inner wholeness, which controls the equilibrium of the *whole* psyche." (1995, p. 165).

As the person moves down the path of self-understanding, the individuation process begins to unfold. The aim of the individuation process is to develop a greater degree of wholeness and more immediate access to the Self. At this depth of psychological awareness, the complexes begin to lose their grip and the person approaches the dark reaches of the shadow where the vantage point of Buddhism provides deep insight—as one embarks on the lifelong journey of self-understanding.

The Shadow in the Service of the Light

The shadow is the dark in all of us, the unconscious, that which is not visible. It is not necessarily the dark as in "evil"—although it can be that—but is more generally to be understood as the dark as the unknown. Jung defines shadow as "the 'negative' side of the personality, the sum of all those unpleasant qualities we like to hide, together with the insufficiently developed functions and the contents of the personal unconscious" (Jung, 1943/1966, p. 66). The balance of opposites allows the light and the dark to exist with consciousness.

As Jung explains, one who seeks consciousness must learn to embrace both the light and the dark: "it is necessary to find a way in which his conscious personality and his shadow can live together" (Jung, 1940/1969, CW 11, para. 132). The seeker begins to look into the shadow to see with compassion where there are unmet needs in the psyche that need to be tended in order that one may more effectively engage the world.

It does no good to suppress the shadow. The more unconscious and denied, the more monstrous the manifestations become. Jung describes the suppression of the shadow: "Unfortunately there can be no doubt that man is, on the whole, less good than he imagines himself or wants to be. Everyone carries a shadow, and the less it is embodied in the individual's conscious life, the blacker and denser it is" (Jung, 1940/1969, CW 11, para. 131). The only way to tame the shadow is to befriend it. Seeing one's limitations, including one's potential for evil, and holding it with one's light or Self becomes the alchemical elixir of the perfect union, the balance of opposites.

The psychology of Buddhism teaches what it means to be truly present with our humanity, both its light and dark aspects, and addresses these parts of self with compassion and wisdom. The psychology of Buddhism pushes depth psychology further by urging the maintenance of daily practice to guide one in the process of deeper self-understanding, to hold what "is" without judgment or condemnation. Through this acceptance of self, the doorway to oneness and unity is opened.

"And then," in the wise words of the Buddhist monk and psychotherapist Jack Kornfield, "we will discover an amazing truth: that with compassion, with courage and dedicated effort, we, like the Buddha, can meet the aggressive forces of Mara and these energies can be transformed" (2008, pp. 208–9). The psychology of Buddhism helps the seeker find peace as she begins to meet her conflicting emotions with a sense of equanimity rather than struggle, panic, and disgust, which are never productive or growthful.

From a Buddhist perspective, three states of mind hinder one's ability to experience happiness: wrong knowing, obsessive desire, and anger. These states of mind are also a part of the dysfunctional thinking that manifests war. To deal with them in oneself is already to take a step toward a more peaceful world.

Wrong knowing is the judgmental mind that so easily creates an enemy out of the "other." In "A Jungian Approach to Human Aggression with Special Emphasis on War," Anthony Stevens explains wrong knowing: "Through shadow projection we are able to turn our enemies into devils and convince ourselves that they are not men and women 'like us' but monsters unworthy of humane consideration" (1995, p. 9). The superior notion that my way is right also feeds wrong knowing, as Stevens explains: "The human propensity to regard one's group as special and superior to all others and to treat members of other communities as if they belonged to another inferior species" (1995, p. 7).

Obsessive desire feeds people's propensity toward war through greed and the insatiable desire for more power. Adler thus asserted that "wherever it is a question of power, no matter how excellent its intentions and goals, it will come up against the will to power of the individual and arouse opposition" (1966, p. 169).

Anger is the most destructive of the three hindering states of mind. It has the potential to destroy one's relationships, one's health, and hinder the possibility for spiritual development. Anger, a secondary emotion covering one's primary emotion of vulnerability, fear, or abandonment is the emotion of war. Robert Thurman explains in his book *Anger* how anger masks fear as a way of self-preservation: "It [anger] is closely linked with fear, the anticipation of pain, in the fear weakens the will to bear the pain or take measures to avoid it, and so cripples the decision to act, making it seem necessary to the frightened person to explode irrationally" (2005, p. 46).

War from its self-righteous perspective will "right these wrongs." As explained by Stevens, "The most dreadful catastrophes occur when the moral complex [suppressed or undeveloped aspects of the personality] forges an alliance with the shadow so as to justify us in perpetrating destructive acts of appalling malignity. This is the hideous phenomenon of 'righteous wrath'" (1995, p. 9). This work looks at the strategies of Buddhism for seeing through the anger to the broken psyche, imprisoned by fear, lying beneath one's anger.

Just as wholeness is not a destination, neither is the individuation process. Both are similar to peeling an onion—when one layer is removed there is still a deeper layer yet to uncover. The onion metaphor does not fully carry the weight of the individuation process, in literal terms an onion would be exhausted of layers, but the individuation process would not be exhausted of layers. As one becomes more mature on her path of individuation, she sees more unity and lives with more wholeness. But it is an upward spiral path, continually teaching and renewing her wisdom to higher layers of understanding.

The layers continue to cycle through and become more and more refined. Intentionally, the individuation process brings one to an experience of a deep-seated unity within the diversity of archetypal energies. Externally, it is nourishing that seed of individuation that enables one to step away from the herd and seek one's own truth and then come back as a part of the unity of the living world. When one sees the interdependence of all, one will begin to see the choice to live with compassion. Jung teaches that by looking at the unconscious through dreams, one can see that there are no clear boundaries as there are with conscious content. Contents of a dream cannot be distinguished from each other, and through this permeating nature one can see a unity in all things.

Jung explains, "The indistinguishableness of its [the unconscious] contents gives one the impression that everything is connected with everything else and therefore, despite their multifarious modes of manifestation, that they are at bottom a unity" (1955–1956/1970a, *CW 14*, para. 660). In the web of connectedness what one does to another one does to herself. In the unforgettable words of the Renaissance poet and Anglican priest John Donne,

No man is an island,
Entire of itself,
Every man is a piece of the continent,
A part of the main.
If a clod be washed away by the sea,
Europe is the less.
As well as if a promontory were.
As well as if a manor of thy friend's
Or of thine own were:
Any man's death diminishes me,
Because I am involved in mankind,
And therefore never send to know for whom the bell tolls;
It tolls for thee.

Jung announced the perennial message that while the Luminous Center of the individual has many voices such as Self, Christ, Buddha, and more, these voices are teaching the same principle: "There is only *one* truth it speaks in many tongues." He goes on, "Our world has shrunk, and it is dawning on us that humanity is one, with one psyche" (1958/1970c, *CW 10*, para. 779). It is through the experience of unity that the action of compassion becomes commonplace.

Compassion: What It Is and What It Isn't

Throughout our research, the authors have found many misconceptions about compassion. Compassion is not just a disproportionate devotion to caring for those in need. In that kind of relationship, individuals are often caught in a codependency in which they give too much without caring for themselves, unwilling and unable to maintain healthy boundaries. In compassion one must first tend to one's own needs. Compassion is not just acquiescing to another's wishes. It teaches responsibility and empowerment by engaging appropriate, healthy boundaries. Compassion can only be present through a healthy psychology which gives rise to effective thinking. Effective thinking comes from self-awareness's healthy self-esteem, and the maintenance of healthy boundaries.

Effective thinking is an assertion of positive values emanating from a psyche that is able to see through the dysfunction of anger, greed, and delusion. If one does not understand and practice healthy boundaries, one can become handcuffed by the psychological neediness of others. When one is enmeshed in another's psychological neediness, one is left drained and overwhelmed.

To experience compassion through life-affirming boundaries, one finds meaning and satisfaction in the depth of experience. Compassion does not disregard one's own life for the lives of others; to do so is codependent and uncentered. To live with compassion—to live in a state of interdependence—one holds oneself and the rest of the world in compassion at the same time. The two must remain in balance; otherwise, the giving and receiving cycle is not circular and not sustainable.

> We mistakenly fear that if we become too compassionate the suffering of others will overwhelm us. But this happens only when our compassion is one-sided. In Buddhist psychology compassion is a circle that encompasses all beings, including ourselves. Compassion blossoms only when we remember our self and others, when the two sides are in harmony. (Kornfield, 2008, p. 32)

It is through psychological and spiritual wholeness that a society becomes effective enough to evoke powerful change in the world, including solutions to conflict that do not include war.

Hillman writes, "If war is normal, then it has been and will always be no matter what we do. If war is inhuman, then we must counter it with humane structures of love and reason. If war is sublime, we must acknowledge its liberating transcendence and yield to the holiness of its call" (2005, p. 214). There is no doubt that war is the standard operating procedure for failed diplomacy, and at times war is resorted to before diplomacy has even been investigated as an option. There has been war and unrest for the entirety of human history. For some, war has become a business.

However, is it rational to conclude that because war has regularly taken place, it always will, no matter what we do? Our study sets out to support the idea that war is the result of lower conscious thinking, and at the point where the collective evolves to a higher state of consciousness, conflict will be resolved differently. As Jung explains, "It is, unfortunately, only too clear that if the individual is not truly regenerated in spirit, society cannot be either, for society is the sum total of individuals in need of redemption" (1957/1970b, CW 10, para. 536). If compassion is a quality that can be learned, as science demonstrates, then if we, as individuals and as a collective people, honor and teach compassion, war will not be so widespread.

In "Contemplative Practices and Mental Training: Prospects for American Education," Davidson et al. (2012, p. 146) declares that "consistent with contemplative insights into mental training, research indicated that qualities such as emotion regulation can be cultivated and can change the mind and brain, much like other skills are learned through sustained repetitive practice that over time leads to automatized habit." They continue, "There is also growing evidence that mindfulness training improves adults' ability to regulate attention and executive function, including orienting attention and monitoring conflict and inhibiting emotionally charged but irrelevant information in novice meditators" (Davidson et al., 2012, p. 148). Davidson, along with other neuroscientists, reports that human beings have the ability to change their brain function, to change what seems to be the emotional default settings in one's mind.

This is another example showing that what one experiences today is not necessarily what will always be; if one chooses to nurture qualities of compassion and empathy, then anger and hateful responses are not permanent. What makes war seem normal is being archetypally possessed by Ares. As more of us develop a deeper understanding of who we are, the collective response to allow Ares this much ownership will no longer work as an acceptable way of being. The bombardment of images that reinforce the appearance of the normalcy of aggression and violence is the challenge to those who are moved to take responsibility for this outdated way of defining conflict. Just as it used to be normal to consider a lobotomy or shock treatment for psychological problems, that perspective has evolved, and these procedures are no longer perceived as beneficial and therefore are no longer practiced.

The Keepers of the Vision of Peace

The more examples of nonviolent action and social change, the more others will be inspired to see nonviolence as a viable force to change the world. There are beautiful examples of those who have countered war, hatred, and violence with love and reason. We have leaders who have shown us that nonviolent action toward civil rights and freedom is possible and powerful. Leaders such as Dr. Martin Luther King, Jr. Mahatma Gandhi, Nelson Mandela, and the Dalai Lama are heroic examples of the profound compassion that dwells in our psyche. The more examples of nonviolent actions that create social change, the more powerful the claim becomes that war is an outdated approach to the resolution of conflict.

In the third explanation of war, Hillman (2005, p. 214) declares, "If war is sublime, we must acknowledge its liberating transcendence and yield to the holiness of its call." This statement is provocative; to say that war is sublime can be compared to seeing an addict's high on heroin as sublime. The high from heroin may briefly *feel* sublime to the addict, yet it is destructive to the addict's physical and mental health, well-being, and relationships. Defining war as sublime creates an unhealthy attachment that eventually reveals itself to the psyche as the illness it is.

We do not tell a heroin addict to embrace the holiness of the call of his addiction. Instead, we invite him to experience rehabilitation in order to see the potential of his life. We teach him to see life beyond the grip of the vice in which he currently lives. Those who are entranced by the immolating qualities of war have fallen slaves to Ares' erotic melodies of power, control, and force. The answer to seeing through this flawed form of ecstasy is not in yielding to some strange notion of liberation that derives from killing and being killed; that is just another unconscious state of severely flawed rapture. But rather, it behooves us to ask in this environment of nuclear weapons why killing and being killed might be regarded as sublime.

Dr. Martin Luther King Jr. as the leading voice of the civil rights movement in the United States, is a prime example of the force of compassion. King led one of the most powerful nonviolent movements that changed the world in the not-so-distant past—a social conflict where Ares for the most part remained in balance. Dr. Martin Luther King Jr. offers hope, but Hillman is cynical.

Dr. King answered the call and led his people to answer that call. King states, "The way of acquiescence leads to moral and spiritual suicide. The way of violence leads to bitterness in the survivors and brutality in the destroyers. But the way of non-violence leads to redemption and the creation of the beloved community" (1986/1992, p. 43). Admittedly Hillman's suggestion that the call goes by unheard is true most of the time. The examples of those who have heeded the call are few and far between. While these examples of nonviolent action bring inspiration and hope to promote a world without war, we are not discounting the fact that war is present, and to some degree may always be present, and often rages from within. In fact, we acknowledge it throughout this study in our attempt to face it with emotional and moral realism. What we are aiming at is a drastic reduction in war being used as an option to deal with conflict.

Conflict will arise, and war often appears inevitable. As impossible as the civil rights movement may have seemed on December 1, 1954, when Rosa Parks, a forty-two-year-old seamstress was arrested for refusing to give up her seat on a public bus to a White passenger, she countered what seemed to be impossible. However slowly, the civil rights movement evolved. Our society has changed.

As stated previously, Hillman argues, "We are unconsciously converts to the hopeful illusion [of a world without war]. But hope itself converts into what it covers, its ever-faithful nighttime companion, despair, and we have been instructed deceitfully, in only the upper half of this truth: Look up; a new day is coming" (2005, p. 217). For Hillman hope is often a mask put on to hide from an underlying despair. Many are blind to the presence of their own despair, deluded into only honoring hope, hope from a savior outside of oneself. This one-sided hope has shunned despair as if despair is shameful rather than natural.

As Freud demonstrated, too often that which is repressed will find monstrous ways of reclaiming its place. Similarly, Jung states, "Mere suppression of the shadow is as little of a remedy as beheading would be for a headache" (Jung, 1940/1969, CW 11, para. 133). Buddhism and depth psychology teach freedom from the deluded hope that Hillman speaks of by following what "is," the light and the dark—hope and despair—to be present at the same time. Hillman (2005) explains that the dichotomy of looking outside oneself to be saved (hope) as a way to escape despair, is not a path which will lead to wholeness. Both hope and despair must coexist with consciousness. Both exist within all of us and there is no way to rid one's life of despair only to balance it with hope.

There is, within humanity, the potential to see these revelations of hope and despair, aggression and cooperation, war and peace, as both sides being essential in the creation of wholeness. It is not in eliminating the shadow that one becomes free, it is in honoring it. In wholeness one's truth encompasses the dichotomy of life, allowing space for all the light and all the dark. Only the balance in humanity can change the current momentum toward the monstrous manifestation of shadow in which we all share.

As more people learn to see their responsibility in developing healthy psyches, there will be less unconscious reacting and more conscious choosing. King taught, "As long as the mind is enslaved, the body can never be free. Psychological freedom, a firm sense of self-esteem, is the most powerful weapon against the long night of physical slavery" (1986/1992, p. 171). This is hope in action, not just for civil rights; this is the hope for all of humanity to rise up and take charge to create in themselves the greatest weapon of all, a world of human beings living with healthy self-esteem. It is up to the individual to create that hope, to embark on that inner journey that Jung calls the individuation process, to know one's Self.

King eloquently explains the power of the inner journey, of knowing one's truth from within: "The Negro will only be free when he reaches down to the inner depths of his own being and signs with the pen and ink of assertive manhood his own emancipation proclamation" (1986/1992, p. 171). Humanity will only be free when each of us reaches down to the inner depths of our own being and signs with pen and ink of assertive humanhood, her own emancipation proclamation. Knowing at the depths of one's soul that all human beings are created equal and all human beings are a part of this human family makes killing and being killed not only an obsolete but, indeed, an obscene substitute for conflict resolution.

Is war simply another dysfunctional way of thinking, as dysfunctional as the earlier oppression of so many people: the African American, Native American, Latino American, Asian American, Jews, women, the poor, and countless other segregated groups? Indeed, in war's gross dysfunctionality and in the human carnage that it entails, war, like prejudice, bespeaks a primitivity in the human mind. It is high time we learn to get the better of it much more often than we presently do. This book is a plea not only for the possibility of doing so but for its necessity.

In another observation about war Hillman writes, "The comfort of sleep cushioned by the teddy bear of innocence is precisely what war awakens us from, and to" (2005, p. 215). The authors of this study argue against Hillman's point. War is no more conscious than "sleep cushioned by the teddy bear of innocence." War and innocence are both unconscious reactions; one is passive, the other aggressive. Neither will provide forward motion for the evolution of humanity; if war were capable of evolving humanity, we would have evolved by now since human history has witnessed roughly 5,000 or more years of war. War persists because of humanity consistently choosing to feed Ares to the point of gluttony in our insatiable pursuit of power.

One of the most devastating sources of conflict and war has been religion. Hillman argues: war "shall remain until the gods themselves go away" (2005, p. 214). In order to be compassionate toward people of other faiths, many will need to move from a literal understanding of their tradition to a more mythic perception. As Karen Armstrong explains, "Each of the world religions has its own particular genius, its own special insight into the nature and requirements of compassion. By making room in your mind for other traditions, you are beginning to appreciate what many human beings, whatever their culture and beliefs, hold in common" (2010, p. 63). With a mythic perception, one's tradition is allowed to evolve. In tolerance, one is not fearful of another tradition; one honors the wisdom it brings to those who follow its creed.

The Individual as the Site of Change

Compassion is innate in some. For many, however, compassion is not a natural aptitude. Science understands compassion to be a skill that can be learned and a skill which requires practice to develop. It is through psychological well-being, the inner pilgrimage into the psyche's depths, that one begins to see from a place of unity, a place where I and thou join in dialogical fellowship—this healthy psychological state of unity nurtures compassion.

To awaken compassion, one must seek her own truth, not necessarily the Christian truth, the Buddhist truth, her parents' truth, or her country's truth—but her own truth. A deep centered knowing of who she is. Joseph Campbell describes what it looks like to seek one's truth: "Each [Knight] entered the forest at one point or another, there where he saw it to be thickest and there was no way or path. For where you are following a way or path, you are following the way or destiny of another" (2007, p. 225). The trials of one's own heroic journey lead to the discovery of who one is. A person must conquer her inner and outer dragons before she is capable of knowing her truth.

This quest for one's own truth engenders consciousness and enables one to see through illusion. It is in the freedom of finding one's truth that one overcomes the likelihood of being deluded by the ego's many illusions. As one travels on her path and begins to see through the illusions set up by her psyche, she is no longer trapped by events that seem to happen to her but that, in fact, she is unconsciously constructing or inviting. Seeing through one's illusion builds space for being aware of the vital choices that until now have been hidden behind a wall, often labeled fate. When the questions are not heard, the results feel predetermined.

Education along these lines can and should begin at an early developmental stage, as developmental theory and research suggests is altogether possible (Crain, 2010). There are unparalleled benefits to teaching our children tools of compassion as part of their primary education. Davidson et al. asserts that "insofar as emotion regulation skills can be trained, improvements in empathic responding to others in need could also follow. Given these considerations, new strategies that promote empathy and pro-social behavior in school settings are needed today" (2012, p. 150). Such a change in education might change people's attitude about violence and war and bring lasting social change. The Dalai Lama concurs, "It is vital when educating our children's brains we do not neglect to educate their hearts, and a key element of educating their hearts has to be nurturing their compassionate nature" (2011, p. 56).

While it is clear that peace is not imminent in our world, the argument of this study is that compassion is a learned skill, and that it has the capacity to balance the energy of the Ares archetype with Eirene, the goddess of peace. This new elixir of the perfect union will transmute to an archetype which sustains peace. What is possible is only what we are able to conceive as possible. In other words, we cannot see or appreciate what we do not believe to be true. It may be difficult for us to imagine a world without war. We propose by way of depth and Buddhist psychology that a compassionate way of being—conflict resolution without war—is the next possible step in our collective individuation process; and that although we may not eliminate war in one generation, or two, or five, we can begin the process of lessening its frequency as we move along the road of our collective evolution.

CHAPTER ONE

The Theory of War and the Case for Peace

Education and Therapy in Action

War has been central to human history since that history began. What is it that draws humanity toward the magnetic power of Ares, the god of war? Since we have the power to annihilate human existence with the push of a button, have we, paradoxically, become less civilized than our predecessors? This chapter looks at war and what, if anything, can be done to eliminate it in the future, and how to limit it in our immediate future (and more and more so as time progresses) through both therapeutic and educational means. War and violence will be explored and explained as being in some substantial measure the result of a spiritual deficit in the collective, and we will ask what education and therapy can do to address that deficit.

Fostering Civility through Legal Means

Through the human love affair with violence, have we created a collective mentality that, ironically, feels disconnected, to some degree, from the collective, bereft of a sense of membership in the human family? The answer to that question would seem to be "yes." We have to a considerable degree forgotten the importance of what Adler called social interest—the feeling of involvement with each other in a social body. Many people have become deconditioned to human suffering, unable to appreciate the scope and intensity of the pain caused by intentional human violence as well as by unconscious choices one makes that promote dolor and destruction.

Indeed, unconscious dynamics are often a conscious part of the strategies some corporations and governments use to further their interests, damaging people and endangering the environment in the name of business and profit, playing on the knee-jerk American tendency to view anything that covers itself in the flag of capitalism as good and socially beneficial. Decisions to destroy a river with toxins, contaminating a water supply for people who live nearby, are an act of violence. It is, in fact, akin to an act of war. Paradoxically, the research shows clearly that the death toll for murder has substantially decreased as human societies have evolved. However, death by profit increases yearly.

For instance, Steven Pinker argues in *The Better Angels of Our Nature* that "states are far less violent than traditional bands and tribes. Modern Western countries, even in their most war-torn centuries, suffered no more than around a quarter of the average death rate of non-state societies" (2011, p. 52). However, has society really become more conscious and less bellicose—more whole—or has humanity simply found subtler ways of fomenting torment?

The consequence of murder is too great for most to commit an actual murder, yet the price tag for inadvertently causing many to be at risk for severe illness because of exposure to inappropriately trashed toxic waste is vague, and it is difficult to hold those who are at fault accountable. According to Michael Brown in *Laying Waste—The Poisoning of America by Toxic Chemicals*, as of March 22, 1979, according to the state health department, 1.9 million residents [of New York] at one time or another had potentially been exposed to notably high chemical levels. After issuing a detailed report on the situation, a spokesperson for the New York Public Interest Research Group called the water supply an "industrial sewer." He blamed such conditions for the high cancer rates there, which rank in the nation's top-10-percent category (1981, p. 123).

Brown goes on to say, ". . . in New England where federal and state representatives have warned that more than 200 community [water] supplies in Connecticut, Rhode Island, Massachusetts, Vermont, New Hampshire, and Maine—two million people—are possibly drinking water poisoned with tetrachloroethylene, a solvent used to thin resins that bond vinyl coating to cement pipes" (1981, p. 121). This is clearly violence inflicted upon people by people, something that could not emanate from a state of higher consciousness.

In Massachusetts, Brown continues, "In the summer of 1979, officials learned that there was an open pit, a dry lagoon, covering about an acre of land in which arsenic was piled in caked white powder several feet thick. So concentrated were the arsenic, lead, and other chemicals that a mere

45 pounds of the soil would be enough to administer a lethal dosage to 100 adults" (1981, p. 121).

These are acts of violence against the earth and human beings. Contaminating a water supply is not less morally odious than massacring a tribe with a machete. Both aggressors hold the same power and share the same intent. The only difference is that former kills over time; the latter, quickly.

Many libraries filled with many books would be needed to adequately describe the atrocious acts of people against our earth and each other as the fallout of toxins contaminates our essential resources. It is higher consciousness that changes the rules, compelling one—with a blessedly innate moral sense that higher consciousness both creates and reveals—to do her best to deliver the highest and best product for people and the environment in acts of cooperation.

Violence, on the other hand, is an action reflecting self-interest rather than a decision based on the good of the whole. It is the dehumanizing of "the other," coupled with the desensitization to violence and the veneration of wealth, which allows human beings to collectively make inhuman decisions which put profit before human life.

The decline of violence as reported by Pinker is, of course, a function of laws which punish specific forms of violence. Obviously, however, they do not extinguish the original aggressive energies. Thus, inevitably, such aggression finds other ways to express itself in what Freud called "the return of the repressed." This is when repressed energies come back to haunt the individual in new ways—more symbolic than the original impulse and therefore more difficult to detect and respond to than the original primitive impulse. When this is the case, corporate violence against individuals can be seen as, in the final analysis, a collective neurosis on the part of the corporate leaders who are devising and carrying out their predatory plans.

If state and private corporations engaged in humane practices not because the law dictates it but because it flows naturally from a higher state of consciousness that members of the corporation have attained, new forms of more symbolically refined and more deadly violence would not emerge to fill the space left by the repressed primitive energies—as they clearly have. In an evolved state of consciousness, state and private corporations would not value profit over human well-being, which is as unevolved a mindset as is the predisposition to war, for both lust and greed turn the individual into an object, an instrument that the oppressor uses to satisfy his colonizing appetites.

Merely legal prohibitions and imperatives can never ensure the triumph of compassion and the defeat of aggressive selfishness. True, cultures have found a modicum of civility in their laws, but they have not become truly wise or ultimately successful at controlling their aggressive impulses and appetites.

Our central contention in this study is that *when empathy and compassion are a part of one's way of thinking—largely through consistent and comprehensive educational and therapeutic programs—we will produce a citizenry that will attain much more mature states of consciousness. Its choices will tend toward much greater natural sustainability for the planet and greater holistic well-being for its human inhabitants.* But in order to consider this question in depth and arrive at viable answers, we must look more closely at the theories and evidence about the inevitability of war in the human experience.

The Root Causes of War

As one begins to interrogate more deeply into the root causes of war, the thoughts of many great thinkers emerge. These portray war as an inescapable part of human existence.

As we have already touched upon, the great psychiatrist and intimate associate of Freud Alfred Adler believed that, above all, the individual seeks superiority over others. The ability to wreak destruction on another is, of course, the surest possible evidence that one has death-dealing and fatefully godlike power over him. Indeed, as with Zeus, Thor, and Ares, scorched earth and a decimated, ravaged citizenry follow from their conquering visitations upon the land. Hillman opines that wars begin inside each of us and are continuously fed: "They begin in the shrill voice in the heart of the people, the press, and the leaders who perceive enemies and push for a fight" (2005, p. 205).

Jeremy Black, in *Why Wars Happen*, points out that what we take as the everyday tensions and conflicts of living in modern society are ultimately nothing other than war in different guises and forms: "war therefore may be little different from organized crime or from riots" (1998, p. 235). Robert Thurman asserts even more sweepingly that "War is but the name for 'organized anger'" (2005, pp. 11–12). Now, it is probable that humans will always toy with anger, aggression, and fear; yet the ultimate fruit of such processes—whether they can be turned into something useful to our growth or deadly in their toxicity—depends upon how one chooses to express these emotions. This, in turn, is directly related to one's degree of psychological and spiritual wholeness.

War is probably, as Thurman says, "organized anger." However, as consciousness grows, organized anger becomes something different than war, something more honest, powerful, and creative. But this requires a psyche matured by years of education and even various therapeutic modalities to aid the process of transforming the fires of anger into creative flames. In such flames are forged new and constructive approaches to harnessing their energy as in an artisan's forge, not destructive flames which ignorantly rage across and lay waste our psychological and political landscapes.

In short, the more integrated and educated one's psyche, the more proactive and positive will be one's responses toward potentially lethal emotions. One simply learns to understand and deal with them in more politically and personally effective—more mature and less infantile—ways.

On the other hand, the masterminds of war enlist soldiers and citizens alike by using the weird allure of fear to sell their wares of war. They turn people into pawns in open conflict with each other through the black magic of fear. "Culturally, organized anger sets the standard for our militaristic, violent lifestyle, modeled by heroes from Achilles to the Terminator" (Thurman, 2005, p. 12). Chris Hedges describes the wars in our time to be run by powerful bullies propagating hate:

> The ethnic conflicts and insurgencies of our time, whether between Serbs and Muslims or Hutus and Tutsis, are not religious wars. They are not clashes between cultures or civilizations, nor are they the result of ancient ethnic hatreds. They are manufactured wars, born out of the collapse of civil societies, perpetuated by fear, greed, and paranoia, and they are run by gangsters, who rise up from the bottom of their own societies and terrorize all, including those they purport to protect. (2002/2003, p. 20)

The Transcendent Function: On the Uses and Misuses of Anger

Anger is a normal human emotion; finding peace is not about eradicating anger from one's emotional playlist but rather learning more effective ways to deal with anger. "Anger is healthy," Thurman reminds us, and "we need anger to right wrongs, overturn social evils, revolt against oppression. Anger is only deadly, sinful, or bad when it is unfair, excessive, or self-destructive. Anyone who tries to control or overcome anger is delusional, trying to be perfect, in the grip of Lucifer" (2005, p. 4). The state of being psychologically whole balances anger with its opposite, love. Psychological wholeness holds anger loosely and responds assertively not forcefully.

Indeed, psychological wholeness in general requires holding and balancing opposites in such a manner. Individuation, the goal of Jungian psychotherapy, aims at creating a third perspective as if it were the apex of a triangle, the two polar opposites forming the endpoints of the base. This third position is one that retains the truths that are enfolded in each polar opposite and then unites them into something wholly new, one that is neither anger nor love but is, in this instance, a sort of realistic familiarity between the two poles as a working arrangement to produce something constructive as the fruit of their dialectical tension. Jung calls this process the transcendent function (1948/1969, CW 8, para. 131–193). It has been powerfully argued that this process—not the archetypes, not the anima and animus, not even the idea of the collective unconscious—is the centerpiece of Jungian psychology (J. Miller, 2004).

The importance of the transcendent function in peaceful conflict resolution should be obvious. For, what is conflict but a potentially explosive dialectical tension? And what is a peaceful resolution of that conflict but a transcendent function that affirms and embraces what is valuable in each of the opposites, synthesizes them, and adds to them in order to create a new perspective that allows for mutual affirmation, mutual edification, and constructive cooperation? Additionally, as an approach to teaching opposites to coexist and, what is more, to be *creative* in that coexistence, the use of the idea of the transcendent function in classroom discourse models not just a behavior but a worldview, the importance of which to students can hardly be overstated.

There are many ways to employ the transcendent function in classroom discourse, but all of them require that the teacher be sensitive to opposing viewpoints and that, whenever possible, she refrains from privileging one viewpoint over another but tries to point out the positives and negatives in both positions. This will not always be possible, of course. One cannot affirm a student's racist beliefs, for instance. Yet, where a question under analysis is complex enough to admit of at least several quite different answers (and, as Dewey [1916] never tired of pointing out—issues *should* be that complex in secondary school settings and up in order to be credible and relevant for students), then it becomes the teacher's task to affirm a given point of view but also to show that there is good reason to hold a different point of view as well.

How crucial this discursive skill is to preparing students to live in a democracy is evident in today's political environment, where this skill is woefully absent among discussants. The typical mode of "interaction" is hardly interactive at all but recriminative, arrogant, and simplistic. The common tactic today has become to caricature and demonize any position that is not one's own creed and that of one's ideological group. Such fractious, lose-

lose forms of civic discourse do not lead to peaceful resolution of conflict but rather breed conflict to such a frightening degree that whether or not American democracy itself can overcome and correct this degeneration of discourse—whether, that is, American democracy can survive its corrosive, divisive effects—has become an open question.

Here, as elsewhere, not only *what* students learn in the curriculum but how, together, they engage with the curriculum and with each other, may prove to be crucial in determining whether or not American democracy has a chance of outliving this century or whether it degenerates into an autocracy or a simple battlefield of warring ethno-sexual tribes out for each other's blood (Gitlin, 1995).

What we are arguing is that alienating, totalizing, and self-righteous forms of discourse are themselves a kind of conversational warfare. They entail holding on tightly to one's anger, through the lens of which one views any and all divergent positions. Difference is registered as danger, not an opportunity to teach and be taught by what Martin Buber (1965) has called one's "dialogical partner," the opposite member of the conversational dyad, who, although differently minded than oneself, need not be one's enemy. Indeed, the possibility that the two members of such a dyad can hold a civil and productive conversation is the basic precondition of democracy.

When viewing the other conversants in complex conversations in an adversarial light entails anger, then what results is a form of emotional suicide, for such anger is like a toxin festering in and then consuming one's entire psychospiritual system. It may even have physical effects in the form of somatoform disorders—what used to be called "psychosomatic diseases." Thurman cautions against the danger of a persistent, intractable anger that takes up residence in one's psyche and refuses to be evicted: "First you recognize that anger in the mind alone is a kind of inner murder, a virtual killing of the other who has angered you" (2005, p. 38). This killing from within is a virtual murder that feels like it is directed toward the other, but is, in fact, a self-mutilating attack.

As this anger grows and festers within, it begins to contaminate other aspects of one's life, whereas resolving anger propels one to move through the challenging situation in order to create change, using the situation to clean up one's boundaries and/or life choices. Then, anger does not necessarily mean the relationship is reconciled; abuse and other price tags may be too severe for the relationship to continue but the anger has served its purpose, boundaries are set, and the relationship or situation is no longer harmful. Anger is healthy when it creates discomfort and propels us forward; anger is unhealthy when it lives inside replaying the past through projection and judgment.

Adler and Hillman suggest that, collectively, war is the projection of what lies inside, and the distance of personal responsibility to the collective outcome turns warfare murder into heroic acts of redemption. Most psychologists and philosophers would agree that war is the outer manifestation of a world filled with human beings who are living with unconscious inner turmoil, a multitude of "inner murders." "War simply repeats on a huge scale the repressed and hate-filled ugliness of childhood," asserts Hillman." We do unto others what was done unto us—twice and thrice over because so long stored" (2005, p. 68).

If war is what Hillman describes, then it may not be the result of people's inherently evil nature but rather a learned behavior or a defense mechanism designed to protect the individual from the psychosis of unresolved pain from childhood. In *The Psychoanalysis of War* Fornari observes: "The paranoiac theory of war therefore affirms that wars break out because real difficulties are dealt with in a psychotic manner. What drives man to war would consequently appear to be not so much his innate aggressiveness, a peculiar wickedness of his, as a sort of madness through which he establishes his earliest relations to his environment, that is, to his mother" (1966/1975, p. 101). Fornari is saying that war is a result of unresolved pain from childhood—war as a product of nurture not nature.

This unresolved pain may be brought on from the child's mother or father, by another caregiver, a bully, or any predatory adolescent or adult who is close to the child. Unresolved pain comes in obvious forms such as physical and verbal abuse, but it also develops through less obvious means such as children who consistently have unmet needs because of poverty, entitled and narcissistic parents, or parents who make their children extensions of themselves. The latter parent essentially sees his or her needs as the needs of their child, thereby ignoring the actual needs of the child, teaching the child her needs are not important. All of this (mis)shapes a psyche into weakness riddled with anxiety and fear.

Most of these children will grow up lacking self-esteem and self-worth. This may manifest in many self-defeating ways, with anger and rage being part of that mix. A culture that harbors pain is, in the last analysis, made up of individuals in psychic pain. To change the collective, each individual must take responsibility for her own unresolved psychological issues.

Freud explained the lust for war as a battle within each of us between two instincts, the urge of Eros to love and the drive to death or destruction of Thanatos. The force of destruction and death is very powerful. The more unconscious one is of the struggle between these two forces for residence in one's psyche, the more Thanatos, the god of death, will find opportunity for manifesting his power. Freud asserted that "if willingness to engage in war is an effect of the destructive instinct, the most obvious plan will be to bring Eros, its antagonist, into play against it. Anything that encourages the growth of emotional ties between men must operate against war" (1964/1981, p. 212). Thus it is that teaching compassion, feeding one's compassion-instinct, will counter the drive toward war.

Native American mythology uses a beautiful metaphor to illustrate Freud's view. A wise chief was walking with his grandson. He says to his grandson, "There is fight going on inside of me. It is a terrible fight between two wolves. One wolf is evil, full of anger, envy, hatred, rage, resentment, greed, and arrogance. The other is good, full of joy, peace, love, hope, kindness, empathy, generosity, and compassion. The same fight is going on inside of you and every other person." The grandson thought about this for a few minutes and asked, "Grandfather, which wolf wins?" The chief replied thoughtfully, "The one you feed." What if we fed compassion more deliberately? Surely, this would entail a more nuanced understanding in the teacher of the emotional life of the child.

Depth Psychology in the U.S. Classroom: Its History and Prospects (1922–2022)

In order to recognize and deal with their own and their students' varied and complex emotions in the classroom with the greatest compassion and authority, part of our call for peace education is that students in colleges of education and in-service teachers in the schools can benefit greatly from some exposure to the depth psychologies, which focus precisely on the study and healthy management of these emotions. Sadly, it is only the very rare college of education that even offers the most basic of courses in depth psychology.

In support of the need for this, there has been a small but consistent and vocal minority of educational scholars, teacher educators, and education-minded psychoanalysts over the last century who have called for teachers at all stages in their careers to receive training in how to recognize and deal with what Salzberger-Wittenberg (1989) aptly called "the emotional experience of teaching and learning" in the classroom; for, as it turns out, there are few situations or sites as emotionally complex as those involving classrooms—virtual or actual—and their many types of educational goals and processes.

This should not be surprising. Who one is as a learner is an integral part of one's overarching life-narrative, one's assessment of oneself as an efficacious individual—or not. It is of considerable significance in one's view of oneself in general whether one sees oneself as "good at learning." Relatedly, how successful or unsuccessful one is in a classroom is a complex mix of personal, familial, cultural, political, ethical, and even spiritual components. Such a mix is bound to be overflowing with the entire range of emotions.

To make matters even more complex, students may not do well in a class because of quite legitimate emotions involving personal, familial, cultural, and political factors that have to do with deficiencies not in the students but in the curriculum, the school, or the teacher. If we wish to educate our children for peace, it is necessary for a myriad of reasons that the teacher be sensitive to the numerous emotional universes that are constellating in a classroom virtually every day, some of them within an individual student, some in the classroom as a body.

This study is situated firmly in that camp of educational psychology that concerns itself with such matters. We contend that the attempt to educate for peace and mature negotiation of disputes will be less likely to succeed without the teacher having some degree of proficiency in recognizing and skillfully dealing with the emotional lives of her students.

First, however, let us look a little more closely into this term "depth psychology" that we have used at numerous points so far. Now is a good time to further develop our understanding of what a "depth psychology" is. This account of depth psychology in the classroom, which will cast light on our present attempt to apply depth psychology to educational processes and venues, begins exactly a century ago with the first assays in applying the then-new findings of the original depth psychology—Freudian psychology, or psychoanalysis—to education.

What Is Depth Psychology?

By depth psychology, we mean any approach to cognition and emotion that takes seriously the notion that subconscious and unconscious processes often have a determining effect on how one consciously experiences and intentionally acts in the world. This is a more contentious claim than it might at first appear to be. For the idea that there even *is* an unconscious has been seriously questioned over the last four or five decades by various sociologists and historians who detect in the very notion merely a quasi-medical artifact—even a clinical fiction—resulting from our culture's self-absorbed preoccupation with individual experience, an obsession that has grown to such narcissistic proportions that it has caused us to reify the unconscious and even revere it as a kind of god (Rieff, 1987).

Yet in his magisterial study of the rise of the depth psychologies over the course of the last 250 years, *The Discovery of the Unconscious*, Ellenberger (1970) surely offers a more balanced approach than one that would just dismiss the idea of the unconscious as psychosocial narcissism or bourgeois self-indulgence. To be sure, Ellenberger readily admits and even supports with exhaustive bodies of evidence the claim that the unconscious, and the elaboration of that notion by Freud, Jung, Adler and their many followers, has undoubtedly been related to larger world-historical developments in Western culture. But then again, what hypothesis—indeed, what intellectual product of any sort—can ever claim to be independent of the historical factors within which it was conceived (Gadamer, 1980)?

However, Ellenberger concludes that despite its historical embeddedness—and in many ways, precisely *because* of it—the hypothesis of the unconscious has on balance been intellectually, clinically, and socially quite fruitful throughout the twentieth century and will probably continue to be so. Fay (1987), Giddens (1991), and Catoriadis (1994) have argued that, despite its undeniable dangers, the late-modern "therapeutic society" offers perspectives and practices that are not only individually healing but also politically liberating.

Thus, in talking of "taking the idea of the unconscious seriously," we mean not necessarily to reify it but to realistically appreciate and appropriate its explanatory power, therapeutic uses, historical significance, and political potential.

According to the Jungian theorist Ira Progoff (1959):

> *Depth is the dimension of wholeness in man.* It is not a level in the psyche literally and spatially; but it is indeed a level in the human organism *in principle*. It is present and it is *deeper* down in the psyche in the sense that it is more fundamental than those mental contents that are in closer relation to surface consciousness and to sensory contact with the outer world. (p. 8; emphasis in original)

The social historian and important critic of both Freudian and Jungian theory Peter Homans has said that to be a depth psychology, a system must meet three criteria:

> It assumes first that the mind is the seat of conflicting forces that are accessible only to disciplined introspection and self-observation; second, that these conflicting forces are mounted on a developmental axis that extends back into early childhood experience and forward into adult life; and third, that this developmental axis is situated in the context of a social environment within

which the a structure of individuality (self, ego, person, I, or the like) exists in a conflictual relationship to social, institutional forces such that the self struggles alternatively to appropriate those forces and to free itself from them. (1999, p. 11)

Putting Progoff's and Homan's portrayals of depth psychology together, it should be clear that it offers ways of understanding and practicing education that honor and nurture students and teachers in much greater complexity and scope than those that—as is the case currently in public education—deal almost exclusively with "surface consciousness," cognitive schemata, or political critique. Such approaches, although necessary and good, do not adequately understand or empower teachers or students in all their emotional, ethical, and spiritual complexity. The depth psychologies do.

An Overview of Psychoanalytic Theory in American Education

Neither classical nor post-Freudian theory has had nearly the effect on the American curriculum that they seemed destined to have in the opening years of the twentieth century. At that time, there were great expectations among such Freudians as Anna Freud, Melanie Klein, Susan Isaacs, August Aichhorn, and Oskar Pfister—all of whom had themselves been educators before becoming psychoanalysts—that teachers, through adequate psychological training and (ideally) the experience of their *own* psychoanalyses, would be able to teach and interact with students in ways that not only conveyed knowledge but would also be emotionally beneficial, even therapeutic, to the students in their care.

Indeed, G. Stanley Hall himself—the recipient of the first doctorate in psychology granted by Harvard, the author of the highly influential study *Adolescence* (1904), the founder of the Child Study Movement, and a widely influential voice in American education—hosted Freud and Jung at Clark University for a series of lectures in 1905. Oskar Pfister, one of the early members of Freud's inner circle of colleagues, called Hall "the celebrated psychologer [sic] of youth and religion who rallied around psycho-analysis at an already advanced age" (1922, p. 173). The potential for cross-fertilization between depth psychology and pedagogy thus appeared great and (so it was thought) would soon blossom in the form of new practices in classrooms across the United States at all levels of instruction. The psychotherapeutic wing of American Progressive education arose out of this hope (Cremin, 1964; Zachry, 1929).

The core idea was simple: the teacher, although certainly not a therapist, should nevertheless learn enough about psychoanalysis to know how to guide students in their interactions with each other, with the curriculum, and with the teacher herself so that their unhealthy inhibitions could be overcome and, at the same time, their libido could be harnessed in socially constructive ways. "From this point of view," wrote Caroline Zachry, the chairman of the Study of Adolescents Division of the Progressive Education Association, in her 1929 work *Personality Adjustments of School Children*, "it becomes the duty of the school to discover the causal elements in the child's conduct and so to guide him that his personality and emotional adjustments will be constructive and thus he will be helped properly to face social situations" (p. 3).

In her *Four Lectures for Teachers and Parents on Psychoanalysis* (1930), Anna Freud echoed this theme when she noted that the educator, no less than the parent, needed to bear in mind that "the task of upbringing, based on analytic understanding, is to find a middle road between . . . extremes—that is to say, to find for each stage in the child's life the right proportion between drive gratification and drive control" (p. 128).

Only a psychologically healthy and therapeutically savvy teacher could truly help the student achieve that balance between the instinctual id and the unforgiving superego that Freud saw as the purpose of analysis—a balance that would enable a person "to love and to work," as he put it, the goal of psychosexual development. Furthermore, the psychoanalytically wise teacher would know how to draw those students who had fallen into the underworld of juvenile delinquency back into the broad and sunlit fold of sociocultural normalcy and productivity.

This notion of "mental hygiene in the schools" (Redl & Wattenberg, 1951) was quite elaborately presented in such superb studies as Oskar Pfister's (1922) *Psycho-analysis in the Service of Education*, August Aichhorn's (1935) *Wayward Youth*, Susan Isaacs's (1932) *The Children We Teach*, Caroline Zachry's (1929) *Emotion and Conduct in Adolescence*, and perhaps most eloquently of all in Redl and Wattenberg's (1951) classic, *Mental Hygiene in Teaching*. Nevertheless, as Hilgard (1987) concluded in his study of the evolution of academic and clinical psychology in the United States, there was at most only an "indirect influence of psychoanalysis on elementary education[;] the direct influence was meager, at least before World War II" (p. 688). In secondary education, where social expectations, economic demands, and academic stakes were higher, the attention to the student's inner life was even less.

After WWII, as the general public witnessed in the faces of the men returning from combat undeniable evidence of just how deeply the psyche could be traumatized, there was a resurgence of interest in depth psychological theories and therapies (Jansz & van Drunen, 2004). Feeding this renewed interest in depth psychology was the fact that America was now becoming home to a cohort of psychoanalytic luminaries who were immigrating in the late 1940s and 1950s from war-ravaged Europe to write and work in universities and clinics across the United States. Some of these psychoanalysts even had particular interest in and messages for educational theorists and practitioners. Peter Blos, Erik Erikson, Fritz Redl, and Bruno Bettelheim were among the most significant of these (Hilgard, 1987).

Despite these powerful influences and personages, however, the effect of depth psychology on education, at least in the public-school classroom, remained surprisingly limited even after WW II in elementary classrooms and even more so in secondary ones. Rather, it was, and continues to be, behaviorism (such as that form of it in Skinner's 1956 work, *The Technology of Teaching*) and cognitive developmentalism (as presented in such texts as Piaget and Inhelder's 1969 classic *The Psychology of the Child*) that have had the greatest effect on the public-school classroom since the end of World War II (Cremin, 1988). It is high time for the depth psychologies to now have their rightful place in education—all the more so if we take seriously the idea of education for peace.

The Jungian turn in depth educational psychology. With the publication of Clifford Mayes' *Jung and Education: Elements of an Archetypal Pedagogy* in 2005, the depth psychological movement took on an added dimension in that Mayes' study was the first book-length study to look at the pedagogical implications and applications of classical Jungian psychology. Although there had been a scattering of articles on this subject before, they were few and not particularly in-depth. Jung mentions educational issues throughout his writing but, again, not in a systematic or in a particularly novel way that psychoanalysis had not already dealt with.

Mayes' work, however, brought the whole lexicon of classical Jungian psychology—including the shadow, anima and animus, countertransference, the archetypes and the collective unconscious, projection, and the transcendent function—to bear upon a wide range of educational issues, especially those in multicultural education, instructional theory, cognitive science, and even forays into the sociology and history of education. In the twenty-seven years since the appearance of *Jung and Education: Elements of an Archetypal Pedagogy*, Mayes has authored, coauthored, or edited eighteen volumes in what has come to be known as "archetypal pedagogy" in addition to almost forty refereed articles on the topic. This present study stands firmly in the newly forming "tradition" of archetypal pedagogy in educational studies.

One of the most important of the psychological dynamics that Jung brought to our attention was the projection of one's own shadow. Through modeling how to avoid this in their own behavior with students as well as teaching students how to withdraw shadow projections in their interactions with each other and with the curriculum, teachers who are wise in the ways of depth psychology can perform an enormous service in promoting peace at every level—from the immediately familial to the globally geopolitical. Let us look at this issue in more depth both because of its own intrinsic importance and because it felicitously exemplifies just how important a role depth psychology can play in promoting peaceful approaches to conflict in the classroom in everything from classroom management to acquiring the skill of seeing opposing points of view in engaging the curriculum instead of simply demonizing and dismissing them.

Teaching Violence

Whereas the goal of the forms of education we are advocating for is peace, other institutions, such as the media, often seem oriented toward teaching just the opposite lesson. Instead of being on an educational journey toward withdrawing our shadow from others and dealing with our own darkness, the media encourage us to export our darkness to others, blame them for all the ills of the world, and then engage in warfare—either symbolic or actual—to eliminate them. Lt. Col. Dave Grossman explains, "The media, which should act to bring us together, serves to pull us apart teaching violence, nurturing our darkest instincts, and feeding the nation with violent stereotypes that foster our deepest fears" (2009, p. 328).

Thanatos, the god of death, like Ares, the god of war, plays on our confirmatory biases and fears by producing (or often simply creating) what it purports to be compelling evidence that the enemy "out there" must be eradicated to save us. Education for peace must draw on the depth psychologies—principally but not only in the Freudian and Jungian traditions—to school us out of this dysfunctional gut reaction.

For, from a Jungian perspective, similar to Freud's view, humanity is both warlike and peaceful, yet Jung emphasizes the balance needed to hold both aspects with proper voice to honor the presence of both sides of human nature. Through the balance of cooperation and aggression, one finds the consciousness to choose a more diplomatic means of dealing with aggression;

rather than being possessed by Ares or Thanatos and reacting with explosive fuel, one takes a more thoughtful, conscious, attitude.

It is not about eliminating aggression and conflict. It is about balancing them with cooperation and compassion—cooperation and its shadow-side conflict must exist side by side to be in harmony. This is clearly demonstrated in Greek mythology. The child born from the relationship of Aphrodite and Ares is Harmonia. The two in union, the goddess of love and the god of war, create balance—harmony.

When the tension to balance these opposites is not conscious, projection forges monstrous creations out of that which has been ignored or feared. As one suppresses her own darkness, she sees darkness in others, protecting herself from her own darkness within. The shadow by nature is that which is not seen; yet the more it is ignored and feared, the greater is the blindness to one's own shadow projections and the more entrenched one becomes in the illusion that those people "out there" are bad.

Anthony Stevens elaborates on this idea: "Through shadow projection we are able to turn our enemies into devils and convince ourselves that they are not men and women 'like us' but monsters unworthy of humane consideration" (1995, p. 9). In projection one sees differences based on fears. Stevens continues: "As devil incarnate, such an enemy is something to be exterminated without remorse. Destroying him becomes the highest duty, a sacrament. War under these circumstances can be regarded not only as just but holy" (1995, p. 10).

The problem lies in both sides being caught by the illusion of being the righteous "good guys" who must deliver justice. Wars begin because both sides believe they are justified. Stevens goes on to say more about this theory: "The phenomenon of shadow projection helps us understand how it is that each side in a conflict perceives the other as more hostile and unscrupulous, and itself as more innocent and peaceful, than either side really is" (1995, p. 10). This superior and self-righteous mind toward one's enemy is made painfully clear through irony in Mark Twain's poem *The War Prayer*:

Help us
to drown the thunder
of the guns
with the shrieks
of their wounded
writhing in pain . . .
for our sakes
who adore Thee, Lord,

blast their hopes . . .
We ask it,
in the spirit of love,
of Him Who is the Source of Love.

(1951, pp. 37, 53-55, 61)

Twain's poem prays that the Lord, who is the source of love, will destroy those who are in arms against us by causing our enemy to writhe in pain. This prayer, ostensibly being prayed in the spirit of love, in fact grotesquely asks for the wretched destruction of the foe. How is love wishing one's enemy to be thrashing in his own pain? The point here is that the superior mind, the one praying, is on the "good guy team," and his foe is the "evil" side.

Hedges concurs with the theory of projection as a means to create the "good guy team" and the "bad guy enemy." Hedges writes: "All groups looked at themselves as victims—the Croats, the Muslims, and the Serbs. They ignored the excesses of their own and highlighted the excesses of the other in gross distortions that fueled the war. The cultivation of victimhood is essential fodder for any conflict" (2002/2003, p. 64).

Projection keeps the story of victim and perpetrator in perpetual motion; it keeps the illusion believable and alive. Marie-Louise von Franz in *Projection and Re-collection in Jungian Psychology*, concludes that "in projection, a piece of one's own personality is transferred to or relocated in an outer object, it is at the same time a loss of soul" (1980, p. 31). It is the dark in one's shadow that is transferred. It is easy to see it in someone else, and the ego then judges another rather than take responsibility for its own pitfalls. Von Franz explains the loss of soul to be a place of unconsciousness, unaware of one's own affect. Jung states, "Consciousness can hardly exist in a state of complete projection" (1983, p. 242).

Projection, or unconsciously seeing one's limiting behavior through another's behavior, is an ingenious way to avoid responsibility and save one's ego from dealing with the pain of facing one's own shortcomings. Projection lives in the shadow; it is gravely unconscious. To honor the shadow is not to allow monsters to manifest but rather to allow the shadow expression to come forward so that the pain which is stored in the unconscious may be released in more effective and creative ways. As one gains consciousness about one's own behaviors, she begins to see her own rage rather than pointing the finger at those out there.

Jung describes how projection looks. "We are still so sure we know what other people think or what their true character is. We are convinced that certain people have all the bad qualities we do not know in ourselves or that they practice all those vices which could, of course, never be our own" (1983, p. 242). In order to see through one's projection, one must take responsibility for the outcomes he manifests in his life, and he can no longer blame someone or something outside of himself for circumstances that seem to keep happening to him.

Projection gives individuals a scapegoat to blame and in return more water from the river Lethe, whose fluids of forgetfulness and avoidance are given to drink to the person who is projecting. By this inauthentic means, she discovers a way of *not* seeing that it is her *own* darkness that is really the issue here. Perhaps it is Charon who is the real chess master, and an unconscious humanity are his willing pawns. Charon's skeletal frame is draped with layers of dark, dreary, moth-eaten rags that flap like handcuffed, clipped wings in the icy mist of the whipping wind. His mysterious dark face issues a hypnotic and seductive invitation: "Drink from the river Lethe and you will need not suffer; for the pain you inflict upon each other will be forgotten—it will be unseen." Charon is selling oblivion, and humanity is buying. But the price may be that we are unconsciously manifesting the underworld here—on earth.

Lawrence LeShan writes, "It has been widely accepted in psychiatric and psychological circles that war is so widespread and popular because it offers a way to redirect our anxieties to a more comfortable target" (1992/2002, p. 76). LeShan goes on to say, "It is the enemy who is evil and to be rejected, not ourselves. We crave scapegoats, targets to absorb our self-doubts, our feelings of worthlessness and hopelessness" (1992/2002, p. 77). Projection is the illusion that allows humanity to call murder "heroic." It is the illusion that allows humanity to accept the atrocities of war as acts of valor, whereas in civilian life these acts are considered evil, sadistic, inhumane, and criminal.

Lt. Col. Dave Grossman, in his book *On Killing* reminds us that "killing is what war is all about, and killing in combat by its very nature, causes deep wounds of pain and guilt. The language of war helps us to deny what war is really about, and in doing so it makes war more palatable" (2009, p. 92). Grossman describes the language of war as the propaganda that is developed for both the soldiers and the civilians to buy into the story of the "enemy," who must be destroyed. Grossman describes the language of war to be fear, but the feelings of fear are framed as love and protection.

War is a way to protect that which we love: our home, our way of life, and our freedom. This language of protection and love pulls on our heart strings. Ashley Montagu writes in *The Anatomy of Swearing*, "Newspapers and men have engineered conflict and war and raised the battle cry against the 'enemy' because there was profit in it. And men will fight to 'defend their country' because they have been made to feel that their way of life, their lives, and the lives of their families are at stake. But in all this there is nothing remotely instinctive" (1967, pp. 77–78).

Fornari describes the enticement of being a soldier and fighting for one's conviction, "War is an experience of love, for it is based on the alienation of the bad parts of the self which are projected onto the enemy, who is consequently experienced as the destroyer of one's love object" (1966/1975, p. 163). Hedges also discusses the confusion with love being the driving force for war: "The initial selflessness of war mirrors that of love, the chief emotion war destroys. And this is what war often looks and feels like, at its inception: love" (2002/2003, p. 159).

In Grossman's book *On Killing*, he describes how for soldiers these atrocious acts in civilian life so easily become normalized as one is subjected to the distressing life of war. An American soldier said about young new soldiers in Vietnam:

> You put those kids in the jungle for a while, get them real scared, deprive them of sleep, and let a few incidents turn some of their fears to hate. Give them a sergeant who has seen too many of his men killed . . . and who feels that Vietnamese are dumb, dirty, and weak, because they are not like him. Add a little mob pressure, and those nice kids who accompany us today would rape like champions. Kill, rape, and steal is the name of the game. (2009, p. 191)

The Role of Education in Promoting Peace: Three Examples

What all of these messages amount to is, in effect, a program of miseducation, one that lures the individual into seeing war as not only inevitable but glorious insofar as it is the final means of imposing one's own worldview onto others. This is considered justifiable by aggressors, of course, since they firmly believe that their way is not only the right way but the *only* right way to see and act in a given situation. Again, education can go a very long way in countering this philosophically indefensible and geopolitically disastrous way of seeing things. We suggest three means of doing so. The first comes from the educational philosopher Maxine Greene (1974) and her idea of "the Cubist Curriculum." The second comes from Jung and his notion of the shadow. The third comes from the educational anthropologist Shirley Bryce Heath (1983).

The educational philosopher Maxine Greene's (1974) notion of a "Cubist Curriculum" answers to the kind of curriculum that is wanted in encouraging students to see that for every complex problem (and often enough for simpler ones, too) there is a variety of ways of seeing the problem and constructing a solution to it. We can benefit from many ways of looking at a problem and working toward a solution. There is not just one right way that justifies the use of force to impose it on others, who may have another, equally valuable, equally efficacious way to approach an issue. Greene proposes that this kind of curriculum be envisioned and implemented as what she calls "The Cubist Curriculum."

In the "Cubist Curriculum," as in Cubist art, one is looking at the same object from various angles simultaneously so as not be tied into a single official interpretation. The purpose is to defamiliarize consensual reality. Reality being multiple since we inhabit what William James (1916) called "a pluralistic universe," our understanding of it must also be polyvalent. This polysemous curriculum, as one might call it, not only encourages but requires students to take different and even contradictory perspectives on topics and to imagine answers which, although they may be negotiated as a collective process to some extent, must, at the end of the day, be appropriated individually by each student in a way that it provides her material that enriches her life-narrative biographically, world historically, and transcendentally.

This notion is at the heart of archetypal pedagogy and it is a superb means of instilling in the child the reality that multi-perspectivalism offers a wide variety of truthful and healthy solutions to a problem that need not involve the imposition of one group's viewpoint over that of another but that, rather, requires that the various viewpoints come into dialogue with each other, this being the very essence of all truly democratic policies and practice.

A second approach to teaching students to deal with differences as the grounds for forging a shared vision, not the cause for declarations of war on each other, stems from Jung's idea of the transcendent function—that is, arriving at a more nuanced understanding and reconciliation of perspectival tensions from a broader point of view and maybe even from higher ontological and ethical ground. The transcendent function "embraces but transcends" polar opposites in an ongoing dialectical process operating in the service of evolution (Wilber, 2000). Through this Hegelian dynamic, an organism—whether it is a single organism or a member of a social organism—is stimulated to move to ever higher planes of vision and action. Jeffrey Miller (2004) reckons this concept the most important one in Jung's work.

From a Jungian standpoint, curricular issues should not typically be treated as simple dichotomies—right or wrong, true or false, normal or deviant. Some issues do cry out to high heaven for judgment, of course. Beyond question is the moral depravity of such things as child abuse and genocide. Most curricular issues, however, are occasions for shuttling back and forth between poles in order to see the ethical legitimacy of each pole (at least, in its own terms) and the insights that lie in various shades of gray in between.

Indeed, the philosopher of the social sciences Brian Fay (2000) has said this is a necessary strategy in any analysis that aims at looking sensitively at a range of worldviews regarding a specific issue. He calls it the "the Principle of Charity." Such an approach poises the student not to strike out and project darkness onto another when he disagrees, but rather to learn from the other's perspective in the service of reconciliation and transcendence.

Were students deeply trained in this art from the earliest years of schooling to the completion of their secondary and tertiary years, we predict that they would be considerably less liable to project their own darkness onto a dialogical other and would be more likely to see and work with multiple worldviews in a shared workspace than battle each other on the bloody fields of conflict—much more likely, that is, to construct than to destruct.

The third educational antidote to the toxins of miseducation that incline us toward violence lies in Shirley Bryce Heath's proposals (1983) in her sociolinguistic study of literacy practices among three different socioeconomic groups of students in Appalachia, *Ways with Words*. Heath argued for turning students in a classroom into "ethnographic detectives" of each other's cultures, their investigations of each other based on whatever curricular topic was up for analysis at that time.

The movie *Remember the Titans* masterfully shows these ideas being put into practice by a wise African American football coach with a team that suffers from a severe "Black"/"White" division among its players. The coach assigns each member an opposite-race member of the team to "buddy up" with throughout the season to research that partner's life. After a rocky start, each team member learns to honor the other's way of being and even to adopt some of its aspects into his own now-psychosocially-enriched life.

The Miseducational Roots of Dehumanization, Nationalism, and Narcissism

The opposite of engaging with a dialogical Other in I-Thou encounter is narcissism. The narcissist fails to regard anyone or anything as a compound of good and bad elements. He either idealizes his object—or devalues it. The object is either all good or all bad. The bad attributes are always projected, displaced, or otherwise externalized. The good ones are appropriated by the narcissist in order to support his "inflated" self-concepts, to avoid the pain of deflation and disillusionment.

Narcissistic thinking creates an illusion to protect the person from seeing his own weakness, fault, or humanness. He builds himself up by finding fault in others and putting others down; yet, at the same time he needs admiration from others to validate his self-worth. Christopher Lasch in *The Culture of Narcissism* observes that a narcissist "cannot live without an admiring audience" (1979/1991, p. 10). This admiring audience is called "narcissistic supply" and is as necessary to the narcissist as the drug is to the cocaine addict. A narcissistic person is fed by narcissistic supply, usually praise, attention, and admiration.

Lasch goes on to say, "Modern capitalist society not only elevates narcissists to prominence. It elicits and reinforces narcissistic traits in everyone" (1979/1991, p. 232). Narcissism rewards success and performance, which, by themselves, are not necessarily bad things. They only become so when they are employed to use and abuse people as pawns in a program—usually a socioeconomic one. A narcissist does not value another human being as a vibrant and variegated creature of illimitable intellectual and ethical potential. Instead, he sees other human beings as objects which will either further his cause or be discarded as valueless if they don't.

Narcissism is on a personal scale what nationalism is on a collective scale. Nationalism as defined by the *Merriam-Webster Dictionary* is "a feeling that people have of being loyal to and proud of their country, often with the belief that it is better and more important than other countries." The roots of nationalism are in xenophobia, and its bitter fruit is an *excessive* patriotism, or chauvinism, which has always been the stuff that wars are made of.

Note, however, that it is not patriotism that is at fault. Loyalty to one's country is a natural impulse and can be laudable. In *Politics*, Aristotle makes it central to his definition of the human being that he is *homo civitatis*: civic man. Cultivating a healthy measure of patriotism in one's children's and students' emotional and ethical makeup can promote civic virtue in them, and this is all to the good. The error resides not in the loyalty to one's country but in the smug sense of oneself and one's country as superior to other countries and their citizenry.

Narcissism precludes empathy. Caught in this syndrome, one cannot see the value of another person. Therefore, the military relies on dehumanizing tactics to train soldiers into killing machines, for we cannot kill that with which we empathize. Teaching and rewarding soldiers to lack empathy, or how to erase what empathy they might have already had, is thus, literally, the order of the day. The military does this primarily by teaching troops that "we" are superior.

Montagu says, "There is no such thing as an instinct or inborn urge to violent behavior of any kind. Men who are given to physical violence are not so by nature but by nurture. Soldiers will shoot to kill and maim others because they believe it is their duty to do so. Violent men learn their violence from the segment of the culture in which they have been conditioned" (1967, p. 77). What is the price tag of training these soldiers to kill? Grossman says, "The presence of aggression, combined with the absence of empathy, results in sociopathy. The presence of aggression, combined with the presence of empathy, results in a completely different kind of individual from the sociopath" (2009, pp. 182–183).

In some ways it is not that difficult to see how nationalism or narcissistic thinking may seep into one's thinking ever so slightly, and then fester, and grow, as the media sell us fear by the truckload in one massive miseducational project. What is needed to counter this program, therefore, is an educational program that conveys opposite messages. Do such educational visions exist?

Indeed they do, and they are to be found in what is called transpersonal educational theory and holistic educational theory. To these theories we will turn after delving a bit more into the nature and treatment of narcissism.

More about Narcissism, with an Introduction to "Educative Acts"

Both narcissism and nationalism, or any extremist view, Left as well as Right, exhibit what developmental theorists call an "inability to decenter." What is decentering and how do we address it educationally?

Decentering means to step outside the rules, roles, ideologies, and interests that are at the very *center* of one's existence to see things from another person's center, where the rules, roles, ideologies, and interests are different from one's own, sometimes very different. Decentering thus requires the cognitively advanced and emotionally stable skill of being able to *relativize* one's fundamental commitments in the face of equally legitimate perspectives. This we must do if we wish to help the child learn to think in ever-more expansive, creative, and inclusive ways and not stay stuck in the quagmire of personally and socially narrow worldviews; for, such perspectives go hand in hand with narcissism.

In the preadolescent years, children tend to view others in terms of whether they are "one of us" or dangerously "different from us"—not just "we" *and* "they" but "we" versus "them." "We," of course, are the center of the universe. "We" are specially favored by God. "We" possess the political and religious truths that reflect the mind of God. "Our" destiny as a nation is unique among nations and we generally have not only the right but the responsibility to compel other cultures and nations to conform to our political and ethical agendas. Those who reside outside of "our" group are evil and dangerous.

According to most developmental theorists, it is a developmental arrestment to stay stuck at this stage (Crain, 2010). Developmentally appropriate curricula require the student to move out of a "mythic membership" mentality ("You can be part of our group only if you buy into our governing myths") into an existentially more nuanced view which sees the relative merits and demerits that are part of almost any system.

Of course, the child's ability to role-shift is more or less limited, typically until later adolescence, when greater role-flexibility has been achieved, assuming that it gets achieved. For according to classical developmental theorists such as Kohlberg (1987), it is simply the case that not many people will fully develop the sociocognitive ability to venture out very far from the constricted radius of convention—that is, "consensual reality." Indeed, the "in-group/out-group" phenomenon with its "ultimate attribution error" ("My group is inherently good, yours is inherently less good and maybe even bad"), which is by now an established fact of social psychology (Devine, 1996), is in full swing here.

The almost gravitational pull of the mores of "my group" is exceptionally strong and one that relatively few people are ever able to see relativistically as just another set of mores in the world's great variety of such social arrangements. In short, the person situated here can take multiple perspectives on roles within his or her defining social structure but is hard-pressed to assume multiple perspectives on that structure itself. Such consciousness is sociocentric.

However, for those relatively few who do begin to attain something of a more "global" vision in this developmental unfoldment, there is broader understanding and richer role-transitivity. The nascent ability to see oneself, others within one's groups, others outside of one's groups, and, finally, even groups themselves from multiple perspectives—this is a momentous sociophenomenological leap. It also seems to be a continuum, with some people able to socially decenter almost at will, others occasionally able to do so, and most seemingly unable to do so. The narcissistic personality disorders are an extreme personal form of the inability to decenter, just as xenophobia is an extreme social form of the same pathology.

"Educative Acts": Role Transitivity among Teachers and Learners

The core of narcissism is the need to feel superior to others. But, when one thinks himself inherently and generally superior to an "other," one feels no need to attend to that other as a human being who might very well possess certain knowledge and wisdom that would contribute to one's own growth as an intellectual, emotional, and spiritual being. Mayes' notion of "educative acts" rests on the assumption that we all are, or have the potential to be, each other's teachers and learners in life's countless contexts and at every level of our being—from the physical to the metaphysical, from the most commonplace tasks to the most burning ethical issues.

Thus it is that, from the simplest practical tasks to the most nuanced spiritual practices, we are, in pedagogical terms, ever in each other's Zone of Proximal Development, to use Lev Vygotsky's term. This means that in almost any group of individuals, there will be an individual or individuals who can serve as a tutor to all the others in understanding and negotiating a certain dilemma or seizing a certain possibility that presents itself to the group. Given the incalculable variety of situations that individuals—from a simple pair of them to large numbers of them—will confront in their shared journey through life's endless assortment of challenges and possibilities, it is probable that they each have insights and abilities to share with their companions. Each can edify each on life's journey.

This view of group dynamics as largely pedagogical thus reaches beyond the classroom's "educational processes"—although its roots are there—and establishes itself as an existential factor in human interaction in general. Mayes has coined the term "educative acts" to indicate both the origin of the term in classroom practices and its expansion to embrace virtually all fields of human interaction. Its assumption that each individual member of a group can take on the role of teacher to the group from time to time is empowering, interactive, and creative.

Thus, in not only *what* is studied in the curriculum but also in the teacher and students modeling what it means to be both a good teacher and student, the idea of educative acts may prove to be an antidote—in both what is taught and how it is taught—to narcissism. In its pathology of excessive self-absorption and its heedless objectification of all others, narcissism emerges as finally an ethical, epistemological, and even spiritual problem that a pedagogy and an ethic of "educative acts" can help to resolve.

Education for Wholeness as a Remedy to Narcissism

The Transpersonal Psychologies of the 1960s and 1970s engendered the Holistic Education Movement. One of the main objectives of most holistic educational theory is to provide a spiritual context within which education can occur without lapsing into dogmatism or advocacy of any particular faith. An excellent way of accomplishing this is through the establishment of deep and authentic relationships; for, in such encounters, one comes face to face with the unique operation of the Ultimate within another individual, just as they come face to face with its unique operation within oneself. This encounter with one's "dialogical other" (Buber, 1965) is the *sine qua non* of holistic education. Relationship is the key.

And for most holistic educationists, the relationship between individuals is not only the centerpiece of the holistic education project; it is also the emblem and justification for the other webs of relationship that comprise holistic education, where everything is seen in relationship to everything else. Nothing could be as healthily decentering and antinarcissistic as holistic education, where nothing exists in isolation but each is a part of the Universal All and the All is uniquely present in every particular "Each." Ron Miller, a founder of the Holistic Education Movement, clarifies:

> The focus of holistic education is on relationships—the relationship between linear thinking and intuition, the relationship between mind and body, the relationship between various domains of knowledge, the relationship between the community and the individual, and the relationship between self and Self. (Miller, 1990, p. 3)

The three types of curricula that ruled both curriculum theory and practice in the twentieth century were (and continue to be in the twenty-first century) (1) curriculum as transmission, (2) curriculum as transaction, and (3) curriculum as transformation. Let us briefly look at how each type of curriculum does or does not contain holistic elements, and thus we will be able to gauge that curriculum's potential to promote peace.

The first type, curriculum as *transmission*, stems from behaviorism. Here, the student simply gives back to the teacher on a standardized test exactly what the teacher told him in class—what, that is, the teacher transmitted to him. There is no room for creativity.

The second type of curriculum is *transactional*. Here, the teacher and students negotiate the meaning and uses of the items in the curriculum. Catering to the relativization of interpretation, this type of curriculum fits nicely into the purview of holistic education, producing students who are constantly being required to relativize knowledge to know other students' perspectives better, not greedily gather up knowledge to use it as a buttress to prop up that student's ego. The curriculum as transaction is an important element of the empathy-oriented curriculum, but it is not everything.

For it is the curriculum that explicitly focuses on helping the student evolve into a compassionate human being that is most relevant in this regard. This kind of curriculum is focused, in other words, on the *transformation* of the student. It is the transactional/transformational curriculum that we are looking for. As we shall see, the Waldorf Schools curricula are the most inspiring and instructive in this regard, for they focus on "the human capacity for self-transcendence as well as self-realization and are concerned with the optimum development of consciousness" (Schutz, 1976).

Obviously, such a curriculum is precisely what is needed to combat narcissism because it cultivates the development of the self not in contradiction to the development of others but in unison with them. Indeed, holistic education maintains that an education that is not liberatory for all is not liberatory for any. If we are not about the business of liberating others, we cannot hope to become liberated ourselves, for as all the world's major religions have proclaimed, there is no liberation for oneself without caring for the liberation of one's fellows. Or as it has been written: "When ye are in the service of your fellow beings, ye are only in the service of your God" (Mosiah 2:17).

In other words, an ego is credible, vibrant, and authentic only to the degree it is tied into a higher ethic of service. Otherwise, the ego is doomed to alienation because it corrodes the heart with the rough salt of selfishness and closes down the soul in the solitary confinements of solipsism. Ron Miller nicely summed up the response of transpersonal psychology to the narrowness of narcissism:

> An underlying assumption of transpersonal psychology is that physical, emotional, intellectual, and spiritual growth are interrelated, and the optimum educational environment stimulates and nurtures the intuitive as well as the rational, the imaginative as well as the practical, and the creative as well as the receptive functions of each individual. Transpersonal psychology has focused attention on the human capacity for self-transcendence as well as

self-realization, and is concerned with the optimum development of consciousness. (1990, p. 58)

Rudolf Steiner's Waldorf Schools exemplify the best of what we consider to be education for self-realization and concern for one's educational companions in the service of that delicate world-historical phenomenon called democracy. Waldorf Education employs many creative processes and products from art, music, dance, poetry, literature, and world religions to teach the topics and convey the standard skills—and more—that children need to master at any given age in conventional public educational settings.

Children study and make both practical and imaginative products, learning to do so in ways that are relevant to their developmental stage, rich in conceptual substance, and keyed to the dynamics of the communal construction of knowledge. The Waldorf student thus learns the standard curriculum but many other things, too, and in a pedagogical environment that valorizes and nurtures their higher nature—their "better angels," to use Lincoln's phrase. This creates "the imaginative basis for creative learning" (Trostli, 1991, p. 335).

A Waldorf site usually has animals in a minifarm to which children attend throughout the day. In this manner, many of the classroom lessons are brought home in tangible ways. The inclusion of such household tasks as baking, sewing, cleaning, and repairing also accomplishes these purposes as it cultivates educationally unconventional aspects of the student and fosters in him a sense of solidarity with people engaged in all sorts of work. This was certainly the Deweyan vision of "vocational education."

Waldorf children often view and comment on each other's artwork as it is displayed around the room without the signatures of the student-artists—this legitimates the children's sense of interconnectedness by deemphasizing the standard public-school obsession with competition (Mayes, 2003, p. 136). Ownership and competition certainly have their place in the classroom, but just as one aspect of life in the classroom, not as its *raison d'être*.

Demystifying War

Is war an addiction? Is the godlike power of taking a life, or controlling the outcome of other human lives, the cocaine that perpetuates the business of war? Does Ares control us? Hedges, in his book, *War Is a Force That Gives Us Meaning*, explains, "The myth of war sells and legitimizes the drug of war. Once we begin to take war's heady narcotic, it creates an addiction that slowly lowers us to the moral depravity of all addicts" (2002/2003, p. 25). Hedges continues:

> The rush of battle is a potent and often lethal addiction, for war is a drug, one I ingested for many years. It is peddled by mythmakers—historians, war correspondents, filmmakers, novelists, and the state—all of whom endow it with qualities it often does possess: excitement, exoticism, power, chances to rise above our small stations in life, and a bizarre and fantastic universe that has a grotesque and dark beauty. (2002/2003, p. 3)

Of course, not everyone associated with the military is addicted to war. However, we feed the romanticizing of war by pouring into the minds of our children, teenagers, and adults heroic images of war through the pictures and stories in the media, classrooms, video games, and more. The martial perspective becomes a conditioned way of seeing and thinking. The conditioned way of thinking becomes the easy choice, the default setting. A default setting becomes very difficult to question.

What is the reason for the alluring fascination with darkness? Would this fascination with the grotesque and dark beauty reduce if human consciousness were being fed a more balanced diet—one not so thick with the macabre and murderous? This seems plausible given the fact that by the age of eighteen, the average American child will have witnessed 200,000 acts of violence and 16,000 simulated murders on television (Hatch, O. G., & Senate Committee on the Judiciary, 1999; Muscari, 2002). James Potter writes, "It is prudent to conclude that media portrayals of violence can lead to the immediate effect of aggressive behavior, that this can happen in response to as little as a single exposure, and that this effect can last up to several weeks" (1999, p. 28).

In an article published in the *Journal of Personality and Social Psychology*, Anderson and Dill reported: "Violent video games provide a forum for learning and practicing aggressive solutions to conflict situations" (2000, p. 789). Another study published in *Psychological Bulletin* also proposes that "the evidence strongly suggests that exposure to violent video games is a causal risk factor for increased aggressive behavior, aggressive cognition, and aggressive affect and for decreased empathy and prosocial behavior" (Anderson et al., 2010, p. 151).

According to *The Guinness World Records 2014*, Grand Theft Auto V was the first videogame to gross $1 billion (Lynch, 2013). Grand Theft Auto V is an action game where the player assumes the roles of three criminals. Players switch between each character to complete missions. Missions include: stealing cars, planning heists, assassinating targets, various sex acts that the player's character procures from a sex worker, strip clubs scenes, use of narcotics, use of alcohol, and driving while under the influence. The staggering sales of Grand Theft Auto V is an example of the possessive hold Ares has on our collective consciousness; the collective is buying because they crave violence.

In an article published in *Pediatrics*, "Gun Violence Trends in Movies," it is revealed that "violence in films has more than doubled since 1950, and gun violence in PG-13-rated films has more than tripled since 1985. Since 2009, PG-13-rated films have contained as much or more violence as R-rated films" (2014). Stanford University Medical School has introduced the "SMART" (media turn-off) curriculum, which demonstrates that if we reduce the use of television, video games, and movies in a child's daily life, a child's aggressive behavior and terrifying image of the world are significantly improved.

Becoming mindful of what one psychically ingests does not mean all video games are bad and should never be played, but we are suggesting that a balanced diet is long past due. Just as vegetables are healthy for the physical body and should be included as a part of every meal, one may also enjoy a small amount of chocolate and still maintain a healthy body. As one feeds the compassion instinct, we feel it inevitable that the desire for violent media will diminish. Naturally, this will be a slow process of evolution. If one chooses to play video games as a way to honor one's shadow, that may very well be a solution that works, as long as it is consumed moderately in a much more abbreviated form. Just as vegetables are an important part of every meal, so too must the component of compassion be a primary source of psychic nutrition.

It is time to take responsibility and educate people about the detrimental effects that violence has on our psyche. Similar to the campaign on drug awareness, understanding the effects of violence will bring about a conversation that evokes consciousness about what one is ingesting. This elevated consciousness will inform and empower individuals about taking responsibility for what they are feeding their psyches—just as they have learned to feed their body in a healthy way.

Grossman and DeGaetano, in *Stop Teaching Our Kids to Kill*, declare, "We are raising generations of children who learn at a very early age to associate horrific violence with pleasure and excitement—a dangerous association for a civilized society" (1999, p. 3). There are countless studies explaining the toxic results of violence, yet there continues to be a continuous stream of movies, video games, and television programming which promote violence. Grossman and DeGaetano thus concluded that "media violence primes children to see killing as acceptable" (1999, p. 7). Grossman and DeGaetano continue, "Since 1982, television violence has increased 780 percent and in that same time period teachers have reported a nearly 800 percent increase of aggressive acts on the playground" (1999, p. 26).

Paulo Freire and a Pedagogy of *Concientización*

This miseducation must be replaced, both at home and in the schools, with what one of the twentieth century's greatest pedagogues, Paolo Freire, called "*concientización*," which translates roughly from the Spanish as "consciousness raising." In a pedagogy of *concientización*, the teacher helps students identify the most salient problems in their life-worlds and then constructs the curriculum around those problems. As a Marxist, Freire as a teacher initially engaged in the standard "ideological critique" that typifies Marxist education. This consists of moving into an educational site occupied by the poor, identifying where the roots of socioeconomic inequity in their lives lie, and then showing the students how to uproot them in order to achieve social and economic equality.

What Freire found, however, was that the problems that he and Marxist theory identified as the students' core problems often did not correspond to what they themselves saw as their primary problems. For the wives in lower SES positions, for example, the problems in their lives did not revolve around (or were not seen by *them* as clearly revolving around) economic issues as a Marxist ideological critique would have them assess their lives. Rather, it was in interpersonal, existentially irrelevant, and demeaning communication with their spouse, male rage, alcoholism, and the ongoing use of physical violence against them that they identified as the causes of their plight as battered women. When Freire reoriented his curriculum for them to deal with *those* issues, he found his students much more emotionally and intellectually engaged with the curriculum and finally applying the result of their researches to changing their life-worlds.

A teacher may take a similarly liberating approach to what to include in the curriculum by focusing on literature and activities revolving around the issues nearest to the student's life-circumstances. Or, if that teacher is given a mandated curriculum by the state, he might help students see subtle messages embedded in what is called the "hidden curriculum" that, for instance, glorify warlike solutions. By identifying these hidden curricular texts and forces, the student is already halfway home to getting the better of them and freeing himself from then. Education then becomes revelatory, stimulating change, not simply a means of occluding and reproducing a current inequitable and inhumane social order.

What we are proposing, then, is a pedagogy that defies all the forces that would transform the student into an object of another person's or another group's agenda—typically a political, cultural, or religious one—and attempts to help the student find himself as a unique individual—that is, as an independent and inquisitive *subject*.

According to the educational philosopher Maxine Greene, such a curriculum may be called a curriculum of *caring* for the student, for it aims at liberating him from those insipid stereotypes that invade his consciousness (mainly through the various media) and establish themselves as the standards by which he must conceive and shape himself. A curriculum of caring wishes to free him from that "false consciousness," as Marx called it, and find his authentic self in his studies and classroom interactions, not be a puppet of a curriculum that serves purposes that would dehumanize him, rob him of his spiritual life, and possibly even cost him his physical life.

The Military-Industrial-*Educational* Complex versus the Cubist Curriculum

This educational imperative to teach the student to recognize and resist attempts to objectify him as a military or industrial quisling becomes all the more pressing in light of a warning issued in 1988 by the greatest of all U.S. educational historians, Lawrence Cremin, in the third of his three-volume, 2,500-page tome—*American Education: The Metropolitan Experience*. In 1961, President Eisenhower in his final address to the nation warned that the growth of a "military-industrial complex" was beginning to pose a clear and present danger to American democracy.

In 1988, Lawrence Cremin, the dean of American educational history, went President Eisenhower one better and said that it was the newly emerging military-industrial-*educational* complex that now constituted the threat. Colleges of education have tripped over themselves running toward ever-bigger grants to research ever-more efficient means of training teachers to train children to become obedient and efficient 'worker-citizens' (Spring, 1980) through the instrumentalities of standardized education—the dystopian assault on democracy through (mis)-education. This is the same educational agenda that prepares students to become military and corporate objects.

How different this is from Dewey's notion that the purpose of education should not be primarily to acquire information but to seek "self-realization" as a free member of a robust democracy. Likewise, Maxine Greene asserted that curricula should offer the student the "possibility for him as an existing person [to make] sense of his own life-world." The caring teacher helps the student identify and realize himself and his project as an "existing person" with "his own life-world."

For Noddings, the pedagogical and ethical imperative is to care: "An ethic of care is thoroughly relational. It is the *relation* to which we point when we use the term 'caring'." Her approach, stemming from a feminist "relational pedagogy," offers the student ample curricular "occasions for ordering the materials of [her unique] world, for imposing 'configurations' by means of experiences and perspectives made available for personally conducted cognitive action" (1995, p. 142). But before reconstructing our world, we must first deconstruct it by exploding the comfortable geometries of our ordinary existence. This aesthetic goal, which underlay Cubist painting, is translated by Greene into educational terms as the "Cubist curriculum."

The purpose of this is to move the teacher and student beyond the easy, standard interpretations of the subject matter; to confront the issues under discussion with the same intensity, curiosity, and creativity with which one confronts a piece of art for the first time. The teacher, no less than the student, must come face to face with the subject matter with the emotional clarity and moral sincerity that a good critic employs in evaluating a piece of art. In doing so, the student and teacher together rout out the seductive imagery of false consciousness to get to the heart of the attempt to objectify the student. These are significant educational moments in helping to free the student from the fatal romances of war and all the covert forces, both in his own shadow and the shadow of his culture, that would lure him into the blood-soaked traps.

War as a Spiritual Problem

War creates a sense of meaning; it feels like patriotic love. It gives people a sense of something important, something bigger than their quotidian existence. "The enduring attraction of war," says Hedges, "is this: Even with its destruction and carnage it can give us what we long for in life. It can give us purpose, meaning, a reason for living" (2002/2003, p. 3).

This sense of meaning and reason for living that Hedges describes can come to take on the aspect of the sacred—a spiritual experience. The warrior is fighting for sacrifice, for honor, for protection, for love. Ehrenreich explains, "To the true member of the warrior elite, every war can be a holy one" (1997/2011, p. 161). It is part of the training and the goal of the military to create warriors who are moved deeply by the cause. Each warrior must buy into the rhetoric of why their side is righteous and the other side is the true enemy. Ehrenreich continues, "If battle is a kind of sacrifice and sacrifice is a kind of birth, we can infer that battle has served at times as a peculiar means of reproduction. Battle makes a warrior out of a boy; and his rebirth as a warrior, no less than his original birth, is marked by the shedding of blood" (1997/2011, p. 158).

The sublime rush from war's adrenaline-laced atmosphere gives meaning to those who accept what Ares preaches. War creates a sense of worth in a cause greater than themselves. "In war men enter an alternative realm of human experience, as far removed from daily life as those things which we call 'sacred'" (Ehrenreich, 1997/2011, p. 12). There is a human need to feel the transcendental nature of being a part of something greater than oneself. While it may be misguided and full of pain, like the abused person who continually returns to the predictability of their abusive relationship, individuals continually return to war as a way to fill their need to be a part of something larger than themselves.

If war fills something that is empty inside for those who perpetuate it, would that not change if more human beings chose to be more whole from a psychological or spiritual standpoint? Hillman states, "There is no practical solution to war because war is not a problem for the practical mind.... War belongs to our souls as an archetypal truth of the cosmos" (2005, p. 214). Hillman contends that a psychological awakening is what is needed to see through the gripping illusion of the godlike power that war creates. Hillman dishearteningly contends that humanity will not do the hard work it will take to break the chains of Ares and learn to avoid, or at least minimize, war. It is the authors' hope and indeed conviction that humanity can evolve beyond its current fragmented state of consciousness and embrace a higher state of being where more effective tools to resolve conflict will be commonplace.

We are aware that this is a heady claim, but, as we hope to show in what follows, it is not without adequate support to lead us to hope that, to some extent at least, it is a claim that can *become realized. However, as always, it will require education to play a key role in its realization.* In what follows in this chapter, we will begin to discuss the grounds for our hope and the plausibility of our vision.

More on War

Heraclitus believed war and all kinds of strife to be a necessary component in the evolution of not only people but also things. He contended that "it should be understood that war is the common condition, that strife is justice, and that all things come to pass through the compulsion of strife. . . . Homer was wrong in saying, 'Would that strife might perish from amongst the gods and men.' For if that were to occur, then all things would cease to exist" (1959, p. 29).

Although our goal is peaceful resolution of strife, we agree with Heraclitus that tension is a necessary feature of those dialectical processes that lead to growth. The point is not to eliminate strife; as Heraclitus says, strife is an essential part of universal evolution. Indeed, as a simple matter of common sense we know that it is through the challenging times in life that one discovers courage, strength, intelligence, and creative strategies—not in the times of ease. As we have already seen, this process has a privileged place in Jungian psychology in what he called the Transcendent Function.

The point is not to eliminate tension in this life. We may hope for a state of perfect happiness with no tension, but that is a beatific condition that we have been reliably informed by many religious traditions has been reserved for us in heaven. Here on Planet Earth, negotiating tension is part of the job description. It is incumbent on each one of us to learn to more effectively use various psychospiritual tools to deal with strife, anger, oppression, destruction, greed, power, and the like. Our argument in this book is that, to the degree that we learn to marshal and employ such tools, war will be turned to less and less as a solution. We do not expect an overnight change.

What we do expect is that such changes would occur gradually but reliably with educational and therapeutic modalities oriented toward that end. As we have asserted throughout this study, there are few things that are nearly as important in educational and therapeutic processes than a frank confrontation with one's own shadow in order to prevent projecting it onto others. It is at educational sites especially, both actual and virtual, that most people may learn, through the topics under analysis in the classroom, about the shadow within everyone, not least of all themselves. There is no surer preventative measure against the projection of the shadow onto others than dealing with this phenomenon in the examination of oneself and others in the course of engaging the curriculum.

From a Freudian perspective, one's destructive side must be either turned inward or outward. LeShan explains, "An inward turn destroys the individual; therefore, war is inevitable until we humans progress to a higher level of development" (2002, p. 12). War is the destructive side turned outward. Would the outcome of war change if humanity understood effective ways to deal with the destructive side that exist inside all of us?

We are suggesting that going to war is not a necessity or instinct of the human soul. Anger, conflict, and aggression *are*, yet those emotions do not need to lead to war. It often feels like there are no other options than war, and at times there may not be. Yet, as more people develop a greater understanding of their own psychospiritual dynamics and learn the technologies of well-being, more options will present themselves because individuals will have expanded their visions and come ever closer to the attainable goal of greater psychological wholeness.

The Fates are not to blame. As Cassius wisely opines in *Julius Cesar*, "The fault, dear Brutus, lies not in our stars but in ourselves." What Cassius is presciently referring to, of course, is our own shadows. Yet it is easier to blame the Fates, than to take responsibility for the pain and unrest that lies concealed within the depths of one's shadow. To contemplate the descent down one's own cobweb-covered staircase, leading to the monster-filled psychological basement of one's shadow, is often much too frightening and can lead to a paralysis of the will. But confront it we must—in appropriate measure and in a gradual fashion—in the consulting room and classroom if we are to deal with our shadow and reduce both the frequency and ferocity of wars.

In other words, our position is that war is much more the result of nurture than nature—a changeable behavior despite war having been a terrible feature of human existence since time immemorial. For, most individuals are not whole; most do not live at peace with their shadow and inner demons. The shadow and inner demons, thus unattended to, will manifest monstrous outcomes in war, colonialism, government corruption, and corporate greed if they are left unconscious. Jung therefore sagely observed that "what is not brought to consciousness will present itself to us as fate" (Jung, 1951/1968, *CW 9 ii*, para. 126).

Being educated, in classrooms and consulting rooms, into how to wrestle with our own demons, we learn compassion for ourselves and others. We learn—and having learned, can teach others, in a healthy multiplier effect—about balance and how to tend that which is dangerously agitated in our unconscious. This project, which is of paramount importance on every level, from the most intimately private to the most publicly global, is *not about eradicating the dark emotions but about healthy ways of expressing them*.

We therefore stress our assumption that most human beings wish to live with peace. Hence, although it will not be an easy task to see through the shadow-drenched illusions and clamoring fears that propel us toward war, it is possible to do so. It is not something that will happen in one or two generations, but it can begin with them and it can evolve to the point that we do believe the light of humanity can be ignited through the process of learned compassion and psychological wholeness. For this to happen, the hard work of the individuation process will have to increasingly become the normal way of life, an organizing center of our educational processes and purposes in our schools and the goal of therapeutic processes that will be made available as a matter of public health, not a luxury for the select few. In this manner, individuals and nations can attain a healthy psychospiritual pulse.

Multicultural Education: Beyond the (Merely) Political

Multicultural education will continue to be an integral part of this process in the schools. But as Mayes and his associates asserted in their 2016 study, *Understanding the Whole Student: Holistic Multicultural Education*, what is needed is a multicultural approach that brings people together and does not drive them further apart with a spirit of contentious differences that must ultimately be the undoing of democracy. As the Buddhist priest and poet Thich Nhat Hanh reminds us,

> The most important work of our generations for our world is to use a new level of introspective insight and self-mastery to break the chain of descent of inherited personal, family, and cultural violence of mind, speech, and body. We cannot bring into this world that real peace so urgently needed by future generations without freeing ourselves from bondage to our inherited anger and its violence. (2001, pp. 3–4)

As must already be quite clear to the reader, this book rests on the assumption that the best educational practices are those that acknowledge and nurture every aspect of a student's being—the physical, emotional, social, cognitive, ethical, and spiritual. If that assumption is correct, then it makes sense that the best approach to multicultural educational issues should also be holistic. However, most books that deal with multicultural education fundamentally do so with an overriding emphasis on the *sociopolitical* nature of these issues. Sometimes their tone is contentious, which tends to exacerbate the culture wars that are raging in our society. What is this sociopolitical approach which, although very important, can be problematic when it is the *only* lens that is used to view multicultural educational issues?

The purpose of the sociopolitical approach is to examine the assumptions that shape pedagogical practices and institutional structures in the schools. For (it is argued) these practices and structures operate in ways that are academically unproductive and politically disempowering for students from lower socioeconomic realms and minority ethnic groups. According to these theorists, these unfair practices sometimes result from a conscious strategy on the part of school people, while at other times they happen in a less conscious way as school people—despite their good intentions—uncritically engage in educational and administrative practices that favor some students and cast others to the margins. But (the sociopolitical approach goes on to argue) whether these teachers, principals, and policy makers are acting consciously or unconsciously, they are more or less ensuring that children from the privileged realms of society will do well and that those from the outer realms will continue to live on the edges of school and society.

Now, although we want to take a much broader approach to multiculturalism in the schools than a political one, we also want to acknowledge upfront that this critique of schooling is powerful, rests on a considerable body of research, and (if it is used as one of many ways of approaching the issue of multiculturalism in the schools) can help us understand how to create more truly democratic forms of education (Kozol, 1991). What is more, the sociopolitical approach casts considerable light on the sad fact that the greatest predictor of how a student will do on college entrance exams is his or her parent's socioeconomic status (Berliner & Biddle, 1995). It would be a mistake to minimize the political side of these issues or sugarcoat the conflicts that they involve.

However, it would be an even bigger mistake to look at multicultural issues *only*, or even *primarily*, in political and "politically correct" terms. A student's cultural identity is much more than a political fact. It is an existential fact—even a spiritual one. By that we mean that it is interwoven throughout his entire being—physically, psychologically, cognitively, and ethically.

Also important to the authors of this book is the idea that multicultural education should not simply be about children from disempowered groups (although, to be sure, it must never lose sight of those students' very special needs and challenges). For, *every* student comes from a culture—or, more precisely, a variety of subcultures—that shape that child and prepare him or her to *see* schools and *be* a student in certain ways. *Every student* is multicultural, and this fact affects *every aspect* of the student's life from the sensorimotor to the spiritual. Multicultural education should aim to engage *every student* at *every level* of his or her existence, and it should provide students many ways to communicate about their different ways of being, seeing, and doing in the world.

In short, *holistic multicultural education is simply good education—and it is for everyone.* This is an especially important fact to keep in mind, it seems to the authors of this book, in a society that is now so extremely diverse as is ours. For students who come from socioeconomically marginalized groups, holistic multicultural education is not only socioeconomically empowering but also physically, emotionally, ethically, and spiritually nurturing. For students who come from privileged groups in society, holistic multicultural education will help them see and respect multiple cultural perspectives, thus expanding their inner world and making them more sensitive citizens in a pluralistic democracy.

Out of Darkness . . . Light

We create heroes like the Terminator, Rambo, and Robocop. We buy songs that have lyrics extolling killing or being killed. The desire to engage these maleficent archetypes suggests that they possess a strong psychological pull, for they resonate with many. Thus, mental health at large is in crisis. The seduction of violent action is minimized when the darkness is honored, allowing the darkness to be an inherent part of human existence, which means darkness is not bad, just a part of who we are. Honoring darkness does not mean we seek to create dark; it means we allow it to be what it is, a part of who we are as human beings.

Curiosity about what one is feeling and why invites opportunities for consciousness to expand. By allowing the darkness a voice, it becomes conscious. It becomes a part of the human experience that is talked about and employed to learn more deeply who we are. Humanity will always wrestle with light and dark, but if we feed light more deliberately into our psyche, we manifest more light in our lives. As the individual changes, the collective will mirror those changes and humanity will, slowly but steadily, begin to generate more light in the world.

CHAPTER TWO

Educating Psyche in Compassion

True compassion can only exist within the framework of a well-balanced psyche. Compassion supports healthy boundaries—put on your oxygen mask first before attempting to help others do the same. As Jack Kornfield puts it in his book, *The Wise Heart,* "Living with compassion does not mean we have to give away all our possessions, take in every homeless person we meet, and fix every difficulty in our extended family and community. Compassion is not co-dependence. It does not mean we lose our self-respect or sacrifice ourself blindly for others" (2008, p. 32). Compassion is assertive, strong, clear, and direct. Compassion feels deeply the suffering of another and strongly desires to alleviate suffering in the world but not at the cost of one's well-being.

Kornfield explains, "When compassion opens in us, we give what we can to stop the war, to heal the environment, to care for the poor, to care for people with AIDS, to save the rain forests. Yet true compassion also loves ourselves, respects our own needs, honors our limits, and our true capacity" (1993, p. 225). It takes healthy self-esteem to honor one's own needs. It takes healthy self-esteem to realize one's own limits and set clear and direct boundaries to protect those limits. Compassion means being deeply human and at the same time honoring one's self and others.

> The Dalai Lama says that giving too much seems to be a disease of the West: The Tibetan word for compassion is *tsewa*, which need not necessarily imply that it is directed to someone else. One can have that feeling toward oneself as well. When you say that someone should be compassionate, there is no connotation that you should totally disregard your self-interest. Compassion,

> or *tsewa*, as it is understood in the Tibetan tradition, is a state of mind or way of being where you extend how you relate to yourself toward others as well. Whatever or whoever the object of your affection, you wish it to be free of suffering. (Davidson & Harrington, 2002, p. 98)

In other words, one intends her life to be well and free of suffering as well as that of her neighbor; these two ideas are practiced symbiotically.

Compassion, like muscle memory and rote memorization, is cultivated through practice. As Ignatieff assures us, "Being human is an accomplishment like playing an instrument. It takes practice" (1985, p. 141). Being human is the practice of feeling deeply the experience of another. Being human is feeling empathetically and acting with compassion to alleviate some part of that suffering. It does take practice for most of us to live and act with compassion because we get caught by our own egotistical neediness. Compassion is not "more right," "smarter than," or "better than" anyone else. Ladner elaborates:

> To feel compassion, you must turn away slightly from your own focus on superficial happiness to sense the true condition of others, honestly facing their pains. This turn is considered the key to expanding awareness from its habitual imprisonment in self-centered states of mind. . . . It is thus an open-hearted empathy for the suffering of others and the wish to free them from it. (2004, p. ix)

Compassion is not only feeling deep sensations of empathetic connection, but also wishing and acting in ways that will alleviate some suffering. It takes consciousness to turn away from one's superficial happiness—or ego desires. Yet it is essential for experiencing accurate empathy and compassion.

A dialogue based in empathy and compassion is not a competition to tell the most compelling story but rather to ask questions of the person sharing to further understand her story. An empathetic and compassionate mind does not think about what to say in response while the person is speaking; they listen with presence. One seeking to connect through empathy and compassion does not tell someone, "It will be ok" or "At least it is not as bad as . . ." Receiving the compassionate and empathetic endowment of another offers validation to the person sharing, enabling the person to feel understood, heard, and valued.

Wiseman defines four qualities of empathy: "Seeing the world as others see it, understanding another's current feelings and recognizing their emotion, staying out of judgment, and communicating that effectively"

(1996, pp. 1162–1167). An empathetic connection is seeking to get inside the other person's experience, to make sense of what it feels like to be them. Ciaramicoli and Ketcham avers that "empathy is our common language, giving voice to the heart's most profound yearnings, eloquently articulating the soul's most anguished questions" (2000, p. 244). Empathy is needed to act with true compassion. Empathy and compassion are qualities that foster connection, safety, vulnerability, and love.

In order to be capable of accurate empathy and compassion, each of us must take responsibility for our psychological and spiritual well-being. Indeed, "the extent to which we've developed even-mindedness largely determines our capacity for accurate empathy. Only when our own minds are even can we accurately perceive and portray others in our lives" (Ladner 2004, p. 120). Wiseman concludes that "self-awareness is a prerequisite to empathy" (1996, p. 1164).

To lack self-awareness is to be stuck in ego consciousness where most choices are colored by that which serves the self. Seeing from ego consciousness is based on an agenda of gaining something. It is not present with the experience of the other because the ego-based agenda limits one's vision. Self-awareness, on the other hand, creates a checkpoint to look at one's motivations and bypass the ego's desire by choosing to be present with the others' experience and connect with them through compassion and empathy.

It is not an easy task to gain enough self-awareness to see through some of the ingenious schemes designed by the deceptive ego, obscuring our vision with denial. This hinders our ability to see accurately. The ego is in a constant state of striving to gain position. The degree of opacity that shades one's awareness of one's own evolving self will be the degree to which she must shine her light making the opaque translucent; the more unconscious the more difficult it will be to see through the ego's schemes, making true compassion and empathy difficult to attain.

It is frightful business to face the powerful ego which strives to protect one's chronic state of comfort—thinking the same thoughts, feeling the same feelings, firing the same neurons in the brain. The ego will do everything in its power to stay in this comfort zone. "Any attempt to increase our compassion involves some courage, as we are stepping out of familiar, self-centered habits and are also facing the sometimes-unpleasant truths about others' suffering" (Ladner 2004, p. 253). When we step into compassion, we are also facing the unpleasant truth of our own struggles and suffering; for, to see the suffering of another, we must see our own.

Karen Armstrong emphasizes:

> Those who have persistently trained themselves in the art of compassion manifest new capacities in the human heart and mind; they discover that when they reach out consistently toward others, they are able to live with the suffering that inevitably comes their way with serenity, kindness, and creativity. They find that they have a new clarity and experience a richly intensified state of being. (2010, pp. 21–22)

Empathy creates bonding; it is feeling with people. Compassion is healthy; it is not enmeshed in rescuing, enabling, or fixing others. Compassion empowers the giver as well as the recipient. Compassion does not stay in toxic or abusive relationships. Compassion and empathy do not please another to avoid conflict or simply mollify another by neglecting her real needs. That would be inauthentic. Compassion fosters self-esteem because one must honor her own needs before she may honor another's. Kornfield expands:

> Compassion is not foolish. It doesn't just go along with what others want so they don't feel bad. There is a yes in compassion, and there is also a no, said with the same courage of heart. No to abuse, no to racism, no to violence, both personal and worldwide. The no is said not out of hate but out of an unwavering care. Buddhists call this the fierce sword of compassion. It is the powerful no of leaving a destructive family, the agonizing no of allowing an addict to experience the consequences of his acts. (2008, pp. 32–33)

Chodron (2006, p. 75) touches on two crucial points regarding compassion. The first is that you are truly compassionate only "to the degree you can work with the wholeness of your being." In other words, to the degree one is able to integrate one's unmet needs as a child or trauma as an adult is exactly the extent to which one will see through one's own limiting beliefs or filters of imbalanced thinking. To gain self-awareness and begin to see through one's limiting beliefs is to begin the journey of an integrated mind which in time will allow one to relate with greater wholeness and even-mindedness.

Through this wholeness one will experience secure attachment to others and be capable of co-equal relationships which include compassion. If one does not integrate her psyche, she will not see with a clear lens. She will be limited in her ability to relate with empathy and compassion. Her communication with others at times may be tainted by judgment, insecurity, and other emotional hiccups that cause division rather than safety and intimacy.

The second point Chodron makes is that a "relationship between equals" is a relationship without pity, judgment, projection, and the many other forms that denial of one's own psychological state may take (2006, p. 75). Pity is a state of superiority, acting from the limiting thinking of ego consciousness. Buddhist philosophy describes pity as a dangerous emotion and the neighbor of contempt. The Dalai Lama helpfully asserts that "compassion should not be confused with pity, which implies a sense of superiority. Rather, in compassion there is an underlying recognition, respect, and sense of concern for the other person. There is no notion of looking down at an unfortunate being" (in Davidson & Harrington, 2002, p. 226).

Buddhist philosophy uses the image of the *bodhisattva* to reflect true compassion—an enlightened being who chooses to give up the peaceful state of *nirvana* in order to bring light to those who suffer in the world. A *bodhisattva* needs to be psychologically whole in order to live with profound compassion; she will not be able to meet the world with such deep compassion without even-mindedness. As laypersons we can aspire to be as compassionate as the *bodhisattvas*, to bring benefit to every living being; as we cultivate consciousness we grow our even-mindedness. As one learns more about her neediness and motivations, these ego needs become less entrenched; and as more opportunity arises for oneness, she sees similarities whereas before she perceived only differences.

A Personal Journey into Compassion

One of the authors of this book, Jacquelyn, reports: "A few months ago, I found myself absentmindedly driving home after a challenging three days saturated in arduous family contentions. My mind was more interested in tenderly nursing my emotional scrapes and bruises than driving the car. I pulled off the freeway seeing a homeless man with a sign that read, 'I want to work.' Not 'I will work' but 'I *want* to work.' It was as if his soul captivated mine. I felt his yearning for work and autonomy. His rough, tanned leather skin creased deeply around his heavy, burdened eyes, he seemed exhausted and ashamed, yet still persisting to get up and fight for a better way to live. I sighed deeply and thought, 'Ah . . . me too.' Tears filled my eyes as I thought: 'I am the same as you. We both *want* to work; we both *want* to be free of our addictions; we both *want* to live with ease and without suffering. We both are pleading to be heard, to be believed in.' The feeling of unity in that moment moved me deeply. I drove on, not alleviating any of his suffering other than my prayers. I simply felt with him."

If we are afraid to be present with our own fear and pain, we will not be able to connect with another in their pain. Compassion walks next to the person in pain allowing the experience to teach the lessons, letting it be exactly what is. Superiority or judgment slip into our minds so easily and imperceptibly that they are often unrecognizable to the self. They serve as a mask for one's unconscious pain, fear, insecurity or other damaging emotions that remain in the darkness of one's unconscious. In order to overcome our fear of pain we must be willing to both experience and convey uncomfortable lessons. It is in the place of discomfort, the place of the unknown, that we challenge our default ways of thinking and find a new way of connecting to the world.

Jacquelyn as a Hospice Volunteer: "Who's Dying Here, Anyway?"
Jacquelyn shares yet another lesson in compassion.

"Becoming a hospice volunteer was outside of my comfort zone, yet I signed up and successfully completed the three-week training class. Self-defeating thoughts ran through my mind. 'What if I say something wrong? What if I don't know what to do? What if I hate it? What if my patient does something gross?' My friend who is a hospice nurse looked at me with disbelief and said, 'Wow, that is all about you! What about your patient who could care less about you because she is trying to understand what it means to die?'

"Her observation hit me like a sledgehammer to the gut. Gasping for breath, I realized I want to see beyond my ego's limited and small perspective. Pushing through my fears and discomfort I visited my hospice patient, Mary, for two hours a week for three years. I intended to make her life better when I spent time with her; to give her an escape by playing her favorite movie, giving her a manicure—*doing* something. I wanted to be a 'good' volunteer, to be the volunteer with loads of compassion.

"As I look back at my development of empathy and compassion, I laugh. The very desire to be 'good' at compassion means I am in a state of serving my ego. After three years of visiting with Mary, whom doctors had given weeks to live when she came under hospice care, taught me that there is nothing to be done when someone is waiting to die.

"Compassion dwelled in seeking to understand Mary's experience—not doing her nails. At the beginning of my experience with Mary she most likely felt unimportant, like her needs were not what mattered to me. I was most likely annoying to some degree, probably to a considerable extent, as I projected the importance of my own needs onto Mary. Mary doesn't care about a manicure or her hair being done. I feel good about doing that for Mary? Well, news flash: that is self-serving!

"Compassion meant learning to be still with Mary, even when it takes an uncomfortably long time, to my mind, for her to finish her sentence. It is uncomfortable for me when she speaks slowly because I am judging her to be less than normal—pity unconsciously arises because she cannot speak as well as I do. My nervous reaction is to finish her sentences for her, making her feel even more alienated and handicapped. I am grateful that Mary was patient with me.

"After about a year I started to really ask myself and think deeply about what it is like to be bedridden and waiting to die? I realized I had no idea, I had no answers for Mary, there is nothing I could offer Mary except for my presence which up to this point had been about my needs not hers. Another sledgehammer to the gut, and my mind's light switched on—Mary needs me to 'be' with her. Learning to be still—to be—taught me to connect; and that is when I began to understand what compassion truly is.

"Over the course of the next two years, Mary and I held hands in silence for hours. I often fed her dinner in silence. She would occasionally speak about her husband who had previously passed. At times, Mary would talk aloud to someone in the room. After many dismissive and empty attempts to convince Mary no one else was in the room—I learned to honor Mary's experience. It was not her dementia; her husband often came to visit. In honoring Mary's experience, we connected more deeply. I began to invite Mary's husband to have dinner with us. I learned to be still as Mary smiled at her husband and enjoyed his presence.

"At Mary's 82nd birthday party we all gathered around her hospital bed, singing happy birthday and eating chocolate cake, Mary's favorite. I was introduced as her best friend to all the friends and family who traveled to see their beloved Mary one last time. After finding my seat across the room from Mary, thinking that was the polite and proper thing to do so the traveling friends and family could sit near her, Mary motioned for me to move next to her bed and she held my hand, like we always did, every Tuesday afternoon. Mary and I were best friends.

"A day I will never forget was six months before she passed. Mary reached over with her clammy, frail, boney fingers and grabbed my hand more deliberately than she had ever done in the past. She entranced me with her thoughtful, penetrating eyes which seemed to embrace my soul. After a moment of silence, eyes still piercing my spirit, she whispered: 'Thank you, for thinking that I matter.'

"What a gift Mary has given me, the gift of feeling compassion and oneness; connecting so deeply the boundaries between her and me became blurred. Mary also gifted me with the passion to continue seeking more of that oneness. I am astounded at the grace and beauty that emanated from Mary's presence. It has changed my life forever."

Compassion as a Way of Living

Compassion fosters a deep inner connection based in love and empathy; it is a spiritual experience. Writes the Dalai Lama: "When compassion, or warmheartedness, arises in us and shifts our focus away from our own narrow self-interest, it is as if we open an inner door. Compassion reduces our fear, boosts our confidence, and brings us inner strength. By reducing distrust, it opens us to others and brings us a sense of connection with them and a sense of purpose and meaning in life" (2011, p. 45).

Being in or seeing the interconnection of all things, oneness, is the cornerstone to acting from a compassionate heart. Kornfield explains, "Compassion is our deepest nature. It arises from our interconnection with all things" (2008, p. 23). Compassion is a place of true understanding, of truly seeing one's humanity, and being with their humanity without judgment. Barasch offers a thoughtful metaphor for compassion: "What if it's not a matter of being generous to you but more that you and I are really two hands of the same being? If I refuse you when you're in need, it's like the right hand refusing to remove a thorn from the left on the grounds that it's the left hand's problem" (2009, pp. 60–61).

Compassion sees the sameness rather than the difference. Compassion seeks to understand rather than fight against. Ladner announces the simple but central truth that "compassion is not about holding to any dogma; it is the human quality that allows us to reach out across differences in race, ethnicity, religion, or nationality, connecting with each other. Compassion is a direct antidote to prejudice and aggression, promoting peace in ourselves and in the world" (2004, p. xix).

Compassion is curious. It comments, saying, "That is a perspective I have never thought about. Please help me understand more clearly how that works for you." Seeking to understand another's perspectives and values is only possible if one is secure in herself, to not be threatened when someone else sees things differently. As such, compassion is nondogmatic.

Thich Nhat Hanh explains, "When one becomes dogmatic, he believes his doctrine is the only truth and that all other doctrines are heresy. Disputes and conflicts all arise from narrow views. They can extend endlessly, wasting precious time and sometimes even leading to war" (1991, p. 211). Freedom and choice come when one is not threatened by differences but curious to understand their meaning from the other's perspective. This curiosity develops into a love for the other person as we truly begin to see who they really are and what moves their soul. We begin with difference and find brilliance.

Compassion is beautiful. It is rich. It is meaningful. It is an essential piece of living wholeheartedly. Compassion is the call to each of us to take responsibility and continually evolve into the best person we can be—who we have been put here to become.

Is Compassion a Learned Behavior? The Science of Compassion

It seems clear that compassion is a positive quality for human beings to cultivate, but can compassion become a learned skill? The current research from the field of neuroscience clearly interprets compassion as a learned behavior as well as asserting that meditation is one of the most powerful tools for cultivating compassion and other balanced neurological states of being. Joe Dispenza, author of *You Are the Placebo: Making Your Mind Matter*, writes: "Meditation is another way to bypass the critical mind and move into the subconscious system of programs. The whole purpose of meditation is to move your awareness beyond your analytical mind—to take your attention off your outer world, your body, and time—and to pay attention to your inner world of thoughts and feelings" (2014, p. 148). Meditation is a tool used to quiet the mind, to impede the nonstop barrage of thinking—to stop the neurons in our minds from firing in the same predictable patterns.

Dispenza continues, "Meditation takes us from survival to creation; from separation to connection; from imbalance to balance; and from the limiting emotions of fear, anger, and sadness to the expansive emotions of joy, freedom, and love" (2014, p. 149). Hence, Austin characterizes meditation as "a process of liberation. It will transform an over-conditioned, self-centered person into a more humane being, one who is actualized, buoyant, and compassionate" (1999, p. 461).

Davidson and his associates comprise one of the leading teams that study the neural basis of emotion and methods to increase equanimity and growth in human beings. Davidson has conducted decades of research on the effects of meditation and brain activity, specifically looking at compassion and empathy as a result of meditation in novice meditators as well as in seasoned meditators. Davidson concurs, "My research on meditators has shown that mental training can alter patterns of activity in the brain to strengthen empathy, compassion, optimism, and a sense of well-being" (Davidson & Begley, 2012, p. xix).

In September 1999, Davidson and his team embarked on a journey with forty-eight volunteers to study how meditation affects the mind and particularly how the left prefrontal cortex is affected, which is the area of the mind where compassion as well as other positive emotions are generated. Before the class began, baseline data were gathered from all the volunteers. After a fairly intense eight-week class and four months of meditation practice, these new meditators were again tested and the results compared with the baseline data. Davidson reports, "Anxiety fell about 12 percent among the people who took the MBSR [Mindfulness Based Stress Reduction] class. . . . The level of left-side activation had tripled after four months" (Davidson & Begley, 2012, pp. 203–204). Enhanced left prefrontal activation means there is a greater opportunity to respond with and feel compassion, empathy, and well-being.

The prefrontal cortex is the part of the brain that plays a significant role in emotion, behavior, and cognitive functions. The left side of the prefrontal cortex is active when positive emotions are felt and experienced, and the right side of the prefrontal cortex is active when negative emotions are felt and experienced. Davidson's research demonstrates that mindfulness meditation training significantly aids the development of stronger left prefrontal cortex activity in the brain.

Resilience is the ability to bounce back after a stressful situation has occurred, the ability to normalize and put one's mind back into a state of peace or equanimity. The greater one's resilience, the faster one's recovery time will be. Emotional resilience is the ability to think of unique strategies to cope with adversity; resilience keeps us from descending into despair. Emotional resilience is a vital contributor to being able to sustain well-being and a positive outlook in life.

For example, if a student fails a test because she did not adequately study, a highly resilient mind might say something like, "I did not spend as much time on this material as I needed. Since Sara seems to understand this material really well, I will ask her to study with me for a couple hours. That way I will have the understanding I need to get a grade I feel good about." A low-resilient thinking process might reach the joyless conclusion that "I really blew it. I will never understand this material. I am going to fail this class." The latter will most likely continue the pattern of poor study habits which will not yield positive results and will most likely perpetuate the downward spiral of not being good enough or smart enough in this subject. Low resilience is a self-defeating way of thinking that fires on the right side of the prefrontal cortex, strengthening the pathways to the right hemisphere.

Mindfulness seems to reset the brain's default connections to fire more often from the left prefrontal cortex. The more these connections are practiced and used, the more the brain prefers responding from the left prefrontal cortex over the right, thus generating more states of emotional resilience, compassion, empathy, optimism, and well-being (Siegel, 2007).

In 1949, Hebb proposed a hypothesis that has since become known as Hebb's Law as explained by a team of scientists from the Center for Neural Science at New York University. "When two interconnected neurons fire at the same time, the synapses between them become stronger, and remain stronger for a long time afterward. This form of synaptic strengthening has come to be called Hebbian synaptic plasticity" (Blair et al., 2001, p. 229). Hebb's law can be summarized by saying that "nerve cells that fire together, wire together." The more the same nerve cells fire together—whether it be left-side optimism and resilience or right-side pessimism and doom—the stronger and more ingrained the wiring becomes. We train our brain to react with the same emotions and feelings that we expect to feel or that we have felt consistently in the past. The brain often becomes addicted to the neurochemical reaction that is produced from the same emotions firing in the brain, making it extremely difficult to perceive an outcome that would elicit a different chemical response.

On either side of the spectrum one can become habituated toward optimism or toward pessimism. Those who seem to have a short fuse with anger, those who suffer from depression, or have feelings of being stuck often habituate more right prefrontal cortex activity and will generate negative emotions more of the time. Many people who suffer from this habitual right brain thinking may be so unconscious of their pre-wired disposition for negativity they do not see the possibility of thinking differently. Dispenza (2014) concludes that redundant thoughts hardwire your brain into a fixed pattern of neurocircuitry.

The ability to follow through with tasks is associated with the left prefrontal cortex, which is also responsible for strategizing creative ways to get a project finished. On the other hand, the right side fires when feelings of inadequacy and being stuck arise. When a person feels a sense of being overwhelmed by a project or discouraged from being able to complete a task, the brain is firing in the right prefrontal cortex. The relationship among depression, negative emotions, and stagnation seems to be connected in a self-defeating cycle that creates stronger stagnation and depression the more the brain fires in the habituated thought patterns. In other words, the more we think about being stuck, the more stuck we become.

In the brain, white matter is the communication center; it has been described by scientists as the subway system of communication for the brain. Bundles of nerves fire electrical impulses to other parts of the brain at lightning quick speeds. Renderings of this part of the brain often resemble electrical storms firing from one round cluster of nerves to the next. R. Douglas Fields, Chief of the Nervous System Development and Plasticity Section at the National Institutes of Health, is a developmental neurobiologist with a long-standing interest in brain development and plasticity. He writes:

> White matter, which lies beneath the gray matter cortex, is composed of millions of bundles of axons (nerve fibers) that connect neurons in different brain regions into functional circuits. The white color derives from the electrical insulation (myelin) that coats axons. It is formed by nonneuronal cells, oligodendrocytes, which wrap up to 150 layers of tightly compressed cell membrane around axons. Myelin is essential for high-speed transmission of electrical impulses. (2010, pp. 768–769)

The more white matter, the more resilient one is to challenges; the less white matter, the less resilient. White matter also has plasticity; it changes as we stimulate our minds with learning challenging new skills. Learning involves changes in strength of synapses in white matter. This suggests the same rewiring principal, new networks are possible when the mind is challenged beyond its habitual way of thinking, and the more the new networks are fired, the faster they become. The reverse is also true: habitual thinking that is not challenged fires consistently in the white matter and those pathways become faster and stronger.

The white matter communicates with the amygdala just as it communicates with other parts of the brain. If the highway system to the amygdala is used often, that pathway will learn to fire at rapid speed. The amygdala is involved with our emotions and motivations; and particularly from a survival standpoint it processes fear, anxiety, and pleasure. "The amygdala is one other part of that higher circuitry which 'decides' if a stimulus event will become either rewarding or aversive" (Austin, 1999, p. 230). It is responsible for habituated or learned responses that fast track to a reaction. The directors of suspense and horror movies prey upon the amygdala of their audiences.

A brain that experiences chronic anxiety or depression has created a more active communication system on the right side of the prefrontal cortex, rather than the left. In this instance the left prefrontal cortex is less active and there are fewer receptors or highways communicating from the left prefrontal cortex to the amygdala. Meditation has been shown to reduce anxiety and depression as well as reduce activity in the amygdala. Meditation provides a healthy reduction in stimulus to the amygdala creating more equanimity more of the time. Davidson & Begley explain:

> One of the most effective ways to reduce activation in the amygdala and orbital frontal cortex is through mindfulness mediation. In this form of mental training, you practice observing your thoughts, feelings, and sensations moment by moment and nonjudgmentally, viewing them simply as what they are: thoughts, feelings, sensations; nothing more and nothing less. By learning to observe nonjudgmentally, you can break the chain of associations that typically arise from every thought. *Ugh, I have to stop worrying about work* becomes *Oh, how interesting that a thought about problems at work has entered my consciousness.* (2012, p. 235)

As we change the way our habituated neurological networks fire, we elicit new chemical responses into our brains. Many of them are very helpful in elevating or eliminating the symptoms of depression, loneliness, fear, and anxiety. Dispenza elaborates on this phenomenon: "Studies show that getting in touch with positive, expansive emotions like kindness and compassion—tends to release a different neuropeptide (called *oxytocin*), which naturally shuts off the receptors in the *amygdala*, the part of the brain that generates fear and anxiety. With fear out of the way, we can feel infinitely more trust, forgiveness, and love. We move from being selfish to selfless" (2014, p. 118).

Many of the right hemisphere thinking patterns may be part of the psychological factors contributing to the sluggish development of human evolution toward a more peaceful existence. How many ideas of genius are stuck behind habituated self-defeating thinking patterns? How many human beings, just struggling to survive, are not creating or fulfilling their potentials? What Henry David Thoreau said almost two hundred years ago is still true: "Most men lead lives of quiet desperation."

Doing More Than Just Surviving Stress

Facing the day only to survive is living with an unhealthy profile of stress. Stress does not foster inspiration and creation. As research has clearly demonstrated, stress is a massive contributor to disease and unbalanced psychological states. According to the Mayo Clinic, common effects of stress include: headache, muscle tension or pain, chest pain, fatigue, change in sex drive, stomach upsets, sleep problems, anxiety, restlessness, lack of motivation or focus, irritability or anger, sadness or depression, overeating or undereating, angry outbursts, drug or alcohol abuse, tobacco use, and social withdrawal (Mayo Clinic, 2021). Dispenza explains, "Stress is one of the biggest causes of epigenetic change, because it knocks your body out of balance. It comes in three forms: physical stress (trauma), chemical stress (toxins), and emotional stress (fear, worry, being overwhelmed, and so on)" (2014, p. 96). Epigenetic change means that different genes are activated because of the stress to the body; be it worry, toxins, or physical trauma—the presence of stress activates certain genes and deactivates others. The opposite is also true—namely, that peace and well-being seem to activate different genes.

Stress is intended to be a short-term solution to danger, the fight-or-flight scenario. Stress is meant to dissipate after safety has been regained. According to the 2015 report, *Paying with Our Health*, stress levels are reported to be trending downward, yet stress still remains at much higher levels than what is considered healthy. Finances are the leading cause of stress in this year's report. Seventy-two percent of adults report feeling stressed about money at least some of the time. Twenty-six percent report feeling stressed about money most or all of the time. Thirty-two percent of Americans say that their difficult finances prevent them from living a healthy lifestyle (Anderson et al., 2015, p. 3).

In 2011 the American Psychological Association reported, "Participants' responses have revealed high stress levels, reliance on unhealthy behaviors to manage stress and alarming psychical health consequences of stress—a combination that suggests the nation is on the verge of a stress-induced public health crisis" (Anderson, *Our Health at Risk*, p. 3). This state of chronic stress creates a world where too many are choosing—often unconsciously choosing—to live in survival mode. In survival mode the body is not functioning at a high level; it does not have the capacity to create and heal because it is constantly on high alert to mitigate the next disaster. No organism in nature is designed to withstand the effects of long-term stress. Yet for the Western lifestyle, stress seems to be the normal operating procedure.

As we have already discussed, the brain is fully capable of rewiring or increasing connections to the left prefrontal cortex. This neuroplasticity works through "*pruning and sprouting* . . . getting rid of some neural connections, patterns, and circuits and creating new ones" (Dispenza, 2014, p. 63). Mental training as defined in this discourse as meditation, quieting one's mind, is one of the tools used for pruning old connections and sprouting new ones. "To quiet your mind would mean that you'd have to declare a 'cease-fire' on all of the automatic neural networks in your thinking brain that you habitually fire on a regular basis" (Dispenza, 2014, p. 149).

This "cease-fire" on the thinking mind during meditation soon brings awareness to the thoughts that arise outside of meditation as well; this awareness or consciousness gives space for choice, to choose out of consciousness rather than reaction or a trained habituated response. This space of quiet awareness is pivotal; this is where the choice to do it differently is made. Thinking the same thoughts will create the same behaviors which will endure the same results. In order to find more peace and well-being, one must change one's mind or thoughts, then the behaviors will begin to change, and then life will hold a different outcome.

Meditation is a tool to help human beings make sense of their past hurt, betrayal, and unmet needs from childhood. It is a tool to find peace with whatever may arise. Siegel speaks of the benefits of meditation which he calls a receptive mind, "When we develop the spaciousness of a receptive mind, we come to see mental activities, including states of mind, as just the activities of the mind. Not the totality of who we are" (Siegel, 2010, p. 209). In a receptive mind, the ego becomes disengaged from the feelings that rise and fall due to emotions. The ego becomes less attached to the outcomes and a prescribed way of being and therefore is less threatened.

The Dalai Lama explains: "Meditation is a process where you try to integrate into your personality what you have learned, so there is less of a gap between what you know and how you act. So perhaps meditation is relevant as a solution to our problem here" (in Davidson & Harrington, 2002, p. 223). Through meditation one may rehabitate one's thinking to develop more left prefrontal cortex activity—a disposition promoting well-being, optimism, and compassion. Through meditation we may increase the number of highways that carry compassion and well-being, by increasing the white matter connecting the left prefrontal cortex to the amygdala, simultaneously decreasing the highways on the right prefrontal cortex to the amygdala, which decreases fear, anxiety, and depression.

Gamma oscillations are brain waves that make manifest a higher level of consciousness and elevated spiritual states. The brain must be quiet to access Gamma waves; these brain waves are highly active when one is in a state of unity, selflessness, and compassion.

Science affirms how compassion is a behavior that can be learned and cultivated through practice. But what does the research say about predisposition; what happens to the children who are born with the DNA of violence, anger, rage, and addiction? The research shows that DNA does not act as fate. Nurture, rather than DNA or nature, is the primary source of behavioral development.

Many of the health conditions commonly attributed in the popular mind to DNA do not actually have a genetic makeup; they are learned behaviors. Whether learned from parents, caregivers, role models, friends, or others, they are nonetheless learned patterns of behavior. "There is no gene for dyslexia or ADD or alcoholism, for example, so not every health condition or psychical variation is associated with a gene. And fewer than five percent of people on the planet are born with some genetic condition—like type 1 diabetes, Down syndrome, or sickle cell anemia. The other 95 percent of us who develop such a condition acquire it though lifestyle and behaviors" (Dispenza, 2014, p. 83). In other words, most of the people who develop genetically carried diseases activate that gene later in life through lifestyle and a concomitant psychological condition. While the gene for a disease may be a part of one's DNA from birth, it is one's lifestyle and emotional well-being that seem to activate or not activate it. "Not everyone born with the genes associated with a condition (say, Alzheimer's or breast cancer) ends up getting that. It's not as though our genes are eggs that will ultimately hatch someday" (Dispenza, 2014, p. 83).

What is it that activates these genes and how do we harness the power to control which genes are activated and which are not? What lifestyles and behaviors contribute to activating these genes?

The Role of Epigenetics

The relatively new science of epigenetics is beginning to unravel some of these powerful ideas. Dispenza explains: "The word epigenetics literally means 'above the gene.' It refers to the control of genes not from within the DNA itself but from messages coming from outside the cell—in other words, from the environment" (2014, p. 92). Nessa Carey, former Senior Lecturer in Molecular Biology at Imperial College, London, who now works in the biotech and pharmaceutical industry, informs us that "epigenetics can be defined as the set of modifications to our genetic material that change the way genes are switched on or off, but which don't alter the genes themselves" (2012, p. 7). Epigenetics is the study of how our inner world, as well as our outer world affects the genes, which become the identity of our bodies.

Epigenetics is teaching us that there are many potentials within our DNA. Scientists believe that we only use about 1.5 percent of our DNA, that the DNA not in use lies dormant waiting for an opportunity to express itself. That is a huge potential waiting to be activated. So in essence, at this point in our understanding, human beings potentially have the power to choose the DNA which becomes the expression of their body (Carey, 2012; Dispenza, 2014).

The more empathy, compassion, and ease in one's inner state, the more the body will live in a state of inspiration and creation. Inspiration and creation are our human right. In this state our aptitudes reach their fullest fruition. James Oschman, who has researched for over fifteen years the structure and function of cells and tissues, and now is working to explore the scientific basis for complementary and alternative medicines, explains that consciousness is a whole body experience: "The molecules of emotion, and their receptors, can be found everywhere in the body, on every kind of cell. The so-called 'neuropeptides' and their receptors were not, as previously thought, confined to the nervous system. Mind as revealed by 'neurochemistry,' had proven to be a whole-body phenomenon. . . . [T]he body is the subconscious mind!" (2006, pp. 23–24).

Oschman and his associates are saying that the subconscious mind lives through the entire body. The body becomes the expression of what lies in the subconscious mind, which explains why meditation would offer such a great benefit both psychologically and physically. Oschman goes onto say, "What is being proposed here is that what we refer to as the subconscious is the sum of the sophisticated intelligence and communications of the vast array of cells and matrices, both neural and non-neural, making up the body" (2006, p. 25).

Joseph Sebarenzi, a Rwandan refugee, in an interview with Marc Barasch, explained his realization that resentment was causing his body harm:

> After the genocide, it was a time of anger. I was thinking all the time, *How do I care for my life but also take care of others who are suffering?* I saw that both were the same thing. The anger and resentment I felt towards those others was killing *my* body. I could have a heart attack and die. . . . I realized reconciliation maybe doesn't come first from the perpetrators but from the victims. . . . They [the victims] should help the oppressors to move from guilt to apology to reconciliation. (2009, p. 244)

Joseph suffered grave loss as a Rwandan refugee, yet in his search for meaning, he found the only way to ease his body was to ease his mind, by forgiving his enemy—by letting go, which seems to be another way of describing peace.

Dispenza agrees that the body is the sum total of all that it harbors: "Every atom, molecule, cell, tissue, and system of the body functions at a level of energetic coherence equal to the intentional or unintentional (conscious or unconscious) state of being of the individual personality" (2014, p. 84). The body is choosing to manifest each of its cells at an energetic level that matches its state of being. If one's state of being is stressed out, one's body will manifest as a stressed-out body; a peaceful inner state will reflect a peaceful body and lifestyle. The research in epigenetics shows that our genes are affected very quickly by our inner state, as well as the state of those around us and the toxins in our environment.

As research has demonstrated for many years, stress, anger, resentment, depression, and other destructive emotions are correlated, at some level, with disease both psychologically and physically. "Epigenetics teaches that we, indeed, are not doomed by our genes and that a change in human consciousness can produce physical changes, both in structure and function, in the human body. We can modify our genetic destiny by turning on the genes we want and turning off the ones we don't want through working with the various factors in the environment that program our genes" (Dispenza, 2014, p. 93). As one learns to change that inner state, to "cease fire" on the normal barrage of self-destructive thinking, one's self-punishment begins to abate while the expression of who we are becomes fuller, brighter, and higher.

This is a powerful concept, and to engage its power, one must develop deep self-understanding and consciousness. Meditation is a doorway to self-knowledge; it is the opening through which one begins the journey within. Meditation creates the cease fire on the habitual neural network, creating an opportunity for change. Those who study epigenetics find identical twins to be of particular interest since they share the same DNA. Carey explains that "even genetically identical individuals are epigenetically distinct by the time of birth, and these epigenetic differences become more pronounced with age and exposure to different environments" (2012, p. 81).

In 2005, a group of scientists working with the Spanish Association Against Cancer Foundation found the following: "Our study reveals that the patterns of epigenetic modifications in MZ [identical] twin pairs diverge as they become older. Differences in epigenetic patterns in genetically identical individuals could be explained by the influence of both external and internal factors" (Fraga et al., 2005, p. 10609). The twins do not activate the same genes; their inner state and experience of the world vary, and those variations create genetic differences. The study concludes, "We also established that these epigenetic markers were more distinct in MZ [identical] twins who were older, had different lifestyles, and had spent less of their lives together, underlining the significant role of environmental factors" (Fraga et al., 2005, p. 10609).

Dispenza concurs: "They [identical twins] don't always manifest the same illnesses in the same way, and sometimes one will manifest a genetic disease that the other doesn't manifest at all. Twins can have the same genes, but different outcomes" (2014, p. 94). The more lifestyle changes the twins had during life, the more epigenetically different the outcomes of their lives became—all with the same genes running through their double helix.

Often the behaviors which are commonly thought of as transferred through DNA such as alcoholism and ADD are often passed from generation to generation, but it is not the genes that carry the trait. It is the modeling from the parent or guardian that results in the trait being passed on. If a child is born of an alcoholic mother but is adopted by emotionally intelligent, stable, nonalcoholic parents, most likely the child will not develop alcoholism because the child will learn, as modeled by her emotionally mature parents, more effective tools for dealing with pain, hardship, adversity, crisis, and other challenging emotions. If the child is raised by her alcoholic natural mother, she has a higher probability of becoming an alcoholic because addictive behavior will be the model for dealing with adversity, crisis, or pain. The child may choose a different source to feed her addiction, such as drugs, shopping, codependency, sex, or one of the many other forms addictions may take; nonetheless, the behavior of alcoholism has been passed down.

Children incorporate actions that they see. They learn to relate to the world through example. In order to stop passing these traits onto our children, we must stop modeling survival mode, overstressed living, anger, rage, addiction, and intolerance; it is our duty as role models to be an example of compassion, empathy, and tolerance.

The trouble remains that many people rear children without making sense of their own psychological traumas and unconsciously pass down dysfunctional attachments and scattered thinking from generation to generation. Conscious parenting is thus a key component in nurturing even-minded and psychologically whole human beings. All of us will grow up with some degree of trauma, shame, and dysfunction. But as more emotionally mature adults begin to take responsibility for that which we leave our children, we will begin to affect the collective archetypes that inform our manifest social programs and practices.

Ervin Staub, Professor of Psychology Emeritus of the University of Massachusetts and founding director of its doctorate program in the Psychology of Peace and Violence, claims that "children who have experienced hostility and abuse rather than love and affection, or little structure or guidance, are likely to become hostile and aggressive. Aggressive children frequently are also ineffective. They do not function well in school; neither are they connected to other social systems. Their orientation to self, to others, and to society are all affected" (in Davidson & Harrington, 2002, p. 178). These children do not magically grow up and become effective. They must acknowledge the deficits in their childhood and make sense of their trauma. What if more children grew up with more role models who exemplified wholeness?

If we expect our children to act with compassion, empathy, respect, integrity, self-care, wholeness, and well-being—we must model these qualities. A parent will not be able to teach her child compassion and unity if she does not understand these stages of consciousness herself. One cannot give what one does not have. If children are raised by parents who do not have compassion for other ethnic groups—their children will most likely not have compassion for other ethnic groups. If a child is modeled rage and anger as a way to deal with adversity, the child will most likely use rage and anger to deal with her adversity or she may choose a mate who uses those abusive behaviors against her.

The often-told adage defines insanity as doing the same thing over and over and expecting a different result. Yet collectively many seem to rear children without tending to their unmet needs and unconscious trauma, in turn, passing destructive thinking and behaviors from generation to generation. Collectively we pass on trauma from generation to generation and at the same time many expect the world to become more peaceful and more humane. Compassion is the cornerstone.

Compassion will arise when more individuals tend to their own unconscious, resolving traumas that lie in the shadows, in turn doing their part to heal the collective trauma. When the tipping point reaches a critical mass and more of humanity is tending each of their unconscious traumas, we will inevitably see a more peaceful world. As parents tend to their unconscious traumas, they no longer pass on the survival-mode, stress-filled life, encompassing emotions such as irritation, anger, rage, and intolerance, to their children. It is in a person's state of psychological wholeness that she is capable of making peace with her past trauma, pain, and current disappointments life has brought. Meditation is one of the tools which can ease this transition of bringing these sometimes very painful emotions to one's consciousness.

Has Science Uncovered a Map to a World That Lives in Peace?

Meditation teaches unity and oneness; it expands our ability to be compassionate because the lines between you and me become blurred—establishing a sense of connection. Seeing and experiencing unity creates a compassionate way of experiencing the world; everyone and everything becomes interconnected. The Dalai Lama teaches that "if we all reflect deeply, we will find that our common humanity is precisely the universal principle that can bind us all together" (Davidson & Harrington, 2002, p. 79). As more of humanity becomes more at peace with their subconscious trauma and conscious pain, the result is more love, more understanding, more connection, more empathy, and more peace. Oschman explains that "our very survival as a species may depend upon methods that can resolve and transcend historic animosities and belief systems and thereby wind down our long history of destructive conflict (2006, p. 21).

Many psychologists, researchers, and scientists agree that achieving a state of unity is an essential piece to wholehearted living. Ervin Staub explains, "Not responding to others' needs represents a closing off of the self. Opening up to others, taking their perspective, considering their needs and responding to them all lead to a continued evolution and growth not only of helping, but also of the self" (Davidson & Harrington, 2002, p. 176).

The Dalai Lama says, "It seems that developing inner values is much like physical exercise. The more we train our abilities, the stronger they become" (2011, p. 56). As the Dalai Lama explains, compassion takes practice, just like our muscles in our bodies. Where do we cultivate compassion in the average daily life? Where do we teach the tools so the average person can see this unity and oneness that is fostered from mediation? We need to do more to educate humanity; well-being does not come from self-seeking enterprises, it comes from seeing the mind clearly. Siegel explains:

> Seeing the mind clearly not only catalyzes the various dimensions of integration as it promotes physical, psychological, and interpersonal well-being, it also helps us dissolve the optical delusion of our separateness. We develop more compassion for ourselves and our loved ones, but we also widen our circle of compassion to include other aspects of the world beyond our immediate concerns. This transpirational awareness gives us a sense of being a fundamental part of a larger world. Physical separations and differences become less paramount as we see that our actions have an impact on the interconnected network of living creatures within which we are just a part. (2010, p. 260)

Meditation has been demonstrated to increase resilience as well as awareness or deeper states of consciousness regarding one's thinking and reactions to the world. Meditation fosters relationships because it allows the practitioner to transcend the illusions of the ego. James Austin expresses, "Advanced meditators appear more sensitive to their own mental and perceptual process" (1999, p. 79). Siegel goes on to say, "Life becomes more vibrant and clear. Mindful awareness feels good, and is good for the whole being and his or her relationships with the world and with others" (2007, p. 78).

This is not to say that meditation is a cure for all neurological unrest. Meditation is a piece of a very intricate tapestry woven together through our psychology and neurology. Yet, research shows meditation to be a very effective tool in creating a more whole and balanced mind which lives in more well-being, more compassion, and more empathy—meditation enhances life. The Dalai Lama has declared after evaluating the research of Professor Richard Davidson and others, "I am hopeful that such research may pave the way for the introduction of compassion training in schools, which could be very worthwhile" (2011, p. 56).

If more people cultivated a more active left prefrontal cortex by practicing meditation, would humanity learn more effective ways to meet challenging situations? As stated in the previous chapter, what is happening inside each individual is a miniature version of what is manifesting collectively. As Austin states, "Start by transforming only one person's brain, and whole societies may then undergo authentic change on a major scale" (1999, p. 3). Therefore, it would seem that if we change the inner state of the individual, the outer conditions in the society at large would also transform.

This is a view that Jung clearly and heartily endorsed. For, although he is often accused of having been apolitical, the fact is that Jung's vision was quite political, although, to be sure, given his commitment to those classical values that have fallen out of favor among postmodernists, his political views have never been widely popular academically because he emphasized the primacy of the individual and abhorred the soul-numbing effects of political collectivism—especially socialism and communism (those darlings of so many twentieth-century academics) but also corporate capitalism (Odajnyk, 1976, p. 48). An astute observer of a world wracked by two cataclysmic wars, Jung had very little faith in claims from either the Right or the Left that political solutions could ever bring about a fundamental psychological reform or true historical progress (Odajnyk, 1976, p. 182).

When Jung addressed political issues, he did so almost exclusively from the standpoint of their psychological causes and consequences, ignoring the economic or ideological components. "Every individual needs revolution," Jung wrote,

> inner division, overthrow of the existing order, and renewal, but not by forcing them upon his neighbors under the hypocritical cloak of Christian love or the sense of social responsibility or any of the other beautiful euphemisms for unconscious urges to personal power. Individual self-reflection, return of the individual to the ground of human nature, to his own deepest being with its individual and social destiny—here is the beginning of a cure for that blindness which reigns at the present hour. (1989, CW 7, p. 5)

Jung's approach is valuable because he examines the psychological aspects of social dynamics, something that many sociologists seem virtually to have forgotten how to do in the last half century or so (Gray, 1996). Nevertheless, it is fair to charge Jung with naivety in ignoring economic, cultural and ideological factors and in insisting that important social changes could be effected in all cases simply by focusing on psychological change (Mattoon, 1985, p. 269). For all that, it is still useful to heed Jung's reminder that for social changes to be deep and durable, there must also be a change in people's hearts and minds. Ours is a time which seems always in search of one social program or another that will magically produce "the great society." In devising our grand schemes for cultural and political transformation, we do well to remember Jung's pointed question, "Does not all culture begin with the individual?" (1989, CW 7, para. 327).

Jung was not alone in his suspicion of collectivism. Freud was equally pessimistic about the "mass psychology" of groups. In "Group Psychology and the Analysis of the Ego," Freud (1957/1923) observed that groups sink to the intellectual level of the least common denominator and are therefore especially susceptible to irrational ideas. Like spoiled children, groups need ever greater physical and emotional stimulation. They are cruelly intolerant of outsiders and slavishly obedient to rulers. Subject to what he called "emotional contagion," groups instinctively revert to infantile states and primitive instincts and will follow whatever leader offers them the most enticing rewards or threatens them with the most dire punishments, Freud felt. "Groups have never thirsted after truth," was Freud's laconic conclusion. "They demand illusions and cannot do without them" (p. 174).

In similar strains, Jung decried the evils of what George Orwell so prophetically portrayed in his anti-utopian novel, *1984*—namely, *groupthink*. Collectivist ideologies are "the greatest temptation to unconsciousness, for the mass infallibly swallows up the individual—who has no security in himself—and reduces him to a helpless particle" (1966, CW 16, para. 225). This "leveling down and eventual dissolution [of the individual psyche] in the collective psyche (e.g., Peter's denial) occasion a 'loss of soul' in the individual, because an important personal achievement has either been neglected or allowed to slip into regression" (1989, CW 7, para. 239). Put people together in large groups and what do you have, asked Jung? Just "one big fathead" (1966, CW 16, para. 4).

Besides, "it is . . . ludicrous to say that the individual lives for society. 'Society' is nothing more than a term, a concept for the symbiosis of a group of human beings. A concept is not a carrier of life. The sole and natural carrier of life is the individual, and that is so throughout nature" (1966, CW 16, para. 224). This notion that societies exist in the minds of their members and not as entities that have some sort of independent existence is characteristic of such phenomenological approaches to sociology as "ethnomethodology" (Garfinkel, 1967) and "symbolic interactionism" (Blumer, 1969).

Thus, Jung's answer—indeed, the answer of most depth psychologists to the question of how to attain peace, both inner and outer, both personal and political—is the same as that given by virtually all great religious leaders in humankind's evolution: by first looking to and reforming one's own heart.

Two Paths to Educating for Peace: Unitive and Dialectical Pedagogies

In this section, we examine two forms of spirituality that we call unitive and dialectical. We believe that each form of spirituality has profound pedagogical possibilities in how we can educate students for peace in the schools, and to do so in ways that are not only constitutionally acceptable but, indeed, are constitutionally protected as long as they are relevant to the curriculum, age-appropriate, and providing that the teacher and school do not privilege or in any other way advocate for one spiritual orientation or religious denomination over any other (Mayes & Ferrin, 2001). Let us begin, therefore, by looking at unitive spirituality and dialectical spirituality in order to reveal their major similarities and differences, with special reference to their implications for a pedagogy of peace. Let us also note right at the outset of this section that both forms of spirituality in the schools can avail themselves of the opportunity to teach meditation in a variety of contexts and across a wide range of subjects from art to physical education and from English to physics (Whitmore, 1986).

A Primer of the Two Spiritualities

Stated very broadly, the goal of unitive spirituality is the absorption of the individual self, which is ultimately an illusory formation, into the absolute Ground of Being. This is primarily the form of spirituality advocated for in the previous section. On the other hand, the goal of dialectical spirituality, which carries equally important possibilities for peace education, is the transfiguration of the mortal person into an immortal person in eternal relationship with God, who is himself a distinct person. We highlight some of the major pedagogical implications of each spiritual orientation, noting both similarities and differences. We conclude by discussing how these two spiritually centered pedagogies can be mutually enriching in meeting the needs of an integrative education in the service of peace.

Unitive Spirituality and Pedagogy

Transpersonal theory began when Abraham Maslow and others came to the conclusion in the late 1960s that psychology needed to go beyond behaviorism, psychoanalysis, and his own humanist/existentialist psychology because they ignored the basic human need for "the naturalistically transcendent, spiritual, and axiological." This he called religion with a little "r," implying that such experience did not necessarily require formal religious commitments. Some form of little-r religion is necessary in terms of psychic health because "without the transpersonal, we get sick, violent, and nihilistic, or else hopeless and apathetic" (1968, p. vi; see also Scotton et al., 1996).

As its name indicates, the goal of transpersonal theory is to transcend the merely personal in order to find a reality that is higher and more lasting than the transitory, "personological" self. Most transpersonal theorists insist upon the need for some form of meditative practice to do this, as indeed we have done in the first part of this chapter. Walsh and Vaughan fittingly call meditation the "royal road to the transpersonal" (1993, p. 47).

One of the most immediate effects of regular meditative practice is what the early transpersonal psychiatrist Assagioli (1965) termed "disidentification from sub-personalities." "One of the most harmful illusions that can beguile us is the belief that we are an indivisible, immutable, totally consistent being. . . . Each [of the individual's many subpersonalities] has a style and a motivation of its own, often strikingly dissimilar from those of others. Each of us is a crowd" (Ferrucci, 1982, pp. 47–48). Exposing the illusory nature of the "self" by meditatively watching one's many ephemeral "selves" rise and fall in consciousness serves to dispel the illusion of a discrete "self." This leads to greater emotional presence and practical efficiency.

Deikman (1982), an early researcher in transpersonal states of consciousness, termed this watching function the "Observing Self," which he capitalized in order to suggest that this "Self" is *personologically* empty and therefore *metaphysically* transcendent. The mediating observer begins to intuit that she is connected to a supraindividual, supratemporal Reality. Indeed, she comes to know not only that she is *related* to this supratemporal Reality but that, ultimately and eternally, she *is* it. The self transcends itself at this point into the realization of its own true nature as the One Transpersonal Self, where, according to the classic Hindu tenet, the individual personality dissolves in the discovery that "Thou *art* That." You *are* the Divine One—your putative "individuality" simply being one of Its many playful, illusory, fictive guises.

As one's life is increasingly lived in the unitive light, there grows a deepening sense of the organic interconnection of self, other, nature, and cosmos as a dynamic unity in which—to use a metaphor from Buddhist psychology—each part reflects all the other parts (Guenther & Kawamura, 2005). Indeed, each part *is* only insofar as it is the reflection of all the other parts—a manifestation of the All.

Miller considers this unitive assumption to be the foundation of holistic education (1988). To *know* and (even more importantly) to *intuit* this unitive wholeness *with* one's whole being and, indeed, *as* one's whole being, is to know the sacred as "the innate tendency to experience the world *whole*. It expresses a reverential oneness, a unity among things" (Nelson, 2000, p. 57). The farthest reaches of our subjectivity open out onto the primal landscape of that which fundamentally *is*, and which is only *in* and *as* an indivisible unity.

The unitive view has been encapsulated for many transpersonal theorists and practitioners in Huxley's statement of "the four fundamental doctrines" of "The Perennial Philosophy," so named because it purportedly summarizes the enduring essence of the world's greatest wisdom literature stripped of doctrinal and cultural differences. The Perennial Philosophy and its most recent iterations insist upon: (1) "The interconnectedness of reality and the fundamental unity of the universe," (2) "the intimate connection between the individual's inner or higher self and the fundamental unity of the universe," (3) "the cultivation of intuition and insight through contemplation and meditation," and (4) "social action as a means of relieving human suffering" (Miller & Seller, 1985, pp. 121–124).

The cultivation of intuition in order to arrive at transpersonal awareness is the crowning transpersonal educational task, requiring what Reinsmith calls an "apophatic" pedagogy" (1992). "Here intuition is independent from feelings, thoughts, and sensations. . . . At the spiritual level intuition moves beyond dualism to experience unity directly. . . . Meditation is a technique designed to quiet the mind so that spiritual intuition can arise" (Vaughan, 1985, p. 185).

Examples of Unitive Pedagogy
Although unitive transpersonal spirituality and theory have been key in defining modern holistic educational theory, its origins go back much farther as Forbes (2003) suggested in a groundbreaking study, positing a genealogy that begins with Rousseau, Pestalozzi, and Froebel and runs through Jung, Maslow, and Rogers. Moffett's (1994) and Miller's (1988) genealogies of holistic education also begin with Rousseau, Pestalozzi, and Froebel but then move through both Tolstoy and the American transcendentalists, culminating in Montessori, Steiner, Dewey, and A. S. Neill. What joins these

somewhat disparate philosophers, psychologists, and social theorists is their shared "insistence on the total growth of each person—physical, emotional, social, intellectual, and spiritual" (Moffett, 1994, p. 9). Despite their shared unitive roots, the many ideologies and practices that comprise the "the *holistic paradigm* [constitute] a fertile, imaginative, and highly diverse worldview which draws upon serious scholarship, authentic mystical traditions, radical politics, and, above all, a genuine search for personal wholeness and a culture that would truly nurture human potentials" (R. Miller, 1990, p. 58).

Confluent Education
In the previous chapter we looked at Rudolf Steiner's Waldorf Schools as excellent examples of holistic education, which lays "the imaginative basis for an intellectual understanding" (Trostli, 1991, p. 9).

Another example of the holistic curriculum is "confluent education" (Brown et al., 1976). Here, the curriculum is seen unitively as "an ecological system" of four concentric circles/domains. Moving from the inner circle outward, these four domains are the intrapersonal, interpersonal, extrapersonal, and transpersonal.

The intrapersonal domain includes psychological issues that affect the student's classroom performance such as self-esteem, and the psychosexual dynamics of the student-teacher relationship. The interpersonal domain deals with "functioning with others—parents, colleagues, students, or other adults in the world" (Brown et al., 1976, p. 11). The extrapersonal domain contains traditional instruction, treating of "the context in which people learn and experience life, both in and out of school. This circle could include the formal curriculum, the structure of the classroom, the school as a system, the community, and the values, both implicit and explicit, of society" (p. 11). Ultimately, these three areas are subsumed in the *transpersonal* domain—a domain that for most holistic theorists rests on some form of *unitive spirituality* (Ferrer, 2002).

Transpersonal Adult Education

Transpersonal education is not only well suited to adults but arguably *best* suited to them. Jung insisted that ideally the person in the second half of life should be engaged in a process of increasing spiritualization, a deepening sense of connection to something that transcends bodily death. "Full ego- or self-transcendence becomes possible only during the adult and gerontological years. . . . [B]ecause of life stage or developmental tasks of living, most individuals do not become concerned with such growth needs until the second half of life or later [when they more fully appreciate the fact that] we are all connected in a common humanity and are part of a larger whole" (Wacks, 1987, p. 52).

Curricula rooted in a unitive vision of the "All" promote "a heightened sense of cosmic clarity, altered perception of space and time, an intuitive grasp of the interconnectedness of all things, and a joyful sense of the ultimate perfection of the universe" (Walsh & Vaughan, 1993). The optimistic view of aging in unitively spiritual education contrasts sharply with the insipid American worship of interminable youth, vulgar sex, and glitzy technology—emphasizing the spiritually creative possibilities that are often most potent as one's physical powers begin to fade (Gellert, 2001, p. 22).

The Zen Teacher
In reflecting on their calling and practice, it is not uncommon for teachers to use spiritual imagery that stems, we believe, from the root-image of "the teacher as an archetype of spirit." These archetypal images are of: (1) the teacher as philosopher, (2) the teacher as a federal prophet of democracy, (3) the teacher as priest, and (4) the teacher as Zen master/counselor/mother (Mayes, 2002). In the salience of this last image of the teacher as an exemplar of Zenlike presence, we see the unitive orientation of many transpersonal approaches to education.

For instance, the transpersonal educationist Reinsmith (1992) maintains that the teacher as a "Witness or Abiding Presence" is similar to the master in a Zen meditation hall and represents the culmination of great teaching. The Zen archery instructor and monk in Herrigel's 1971 classic, *Zen and the Art of Archery*, is such a teacher. As the enlightened still-point for the student in her turning world of psychological and moral confusion, this kind of teacher functions as a flawless mirror for the student, reflecting her to herself with such accuracy that she sees herself as if for the first time.

But, paradoxically, seeing oneself clearly is to see that one does not really *have* a *self* at all—just shifting phenomenological responses to shifting conditions. Indeed, the student discovers that there really is no space between the responses and the conditions, for they ultimately dissolve into an immanent merger of consciousness and its illusory objects.

Looking into the mirror of the teacher, the student discovers that the mirror is empty. The teacher has drawn the novice out of her illusory mental formations into that fruitful Void which is self-existent Being. "Teaching in this sense becomes mysterious; the teacher's 'non-doing' paradoxically brings a feeling of fulfillment unlike that in the previous forms. . . . The teacher is moving toward a certain egolessness" (Reinsmith 1992, p. 140). Most transpersonal educationists quite justifiably point to this psychospiritual presence as one of the finest fruits of unitively spiritual approaches to education (Tremmel, 1993).

Dialectical Spirituality and Pedagogy

Unlike unitive spirituality, dialectical spirituality aspires to the transformation of one's *mortal* personal self into an *immortal* personal self in eternal *dialogue* with a *personal God*. Thus, we call it "dialectical." The God of dialectical spirituality is an Eternal Individual, separate from mortal individuals. Nevertheless, he loves and claims each human being because each one is his unique child, engendered in his image. This is true of no other creature—despite their beauty, dignity and importance.

It is God's love for his children that bridges what would otherwise be a fatal gap between him and them. For to some degree or other, all of them will use their free agency in the course of their learning and testing period on this earth to deny their eternal Father's law and love. To mend this rift between a God and children who have alienated themselves through bad choices, each dialectical religion has some sacrificial means that God—out of parental love, knowing that his children were bound to err in their educative sojourn in mortality—has himself provided.

These compensatory means allow God's mercy to satisfy the claims of justice without in any way denying those claims, which, as the God of justice, he *could not* shortchange and still remain true to his nature. Through both the divinely appointed sacrifice as well as the individual's own effort (revivified by the experience of God's forgiveness), the person emerges stronger and wiser, having learned in this realm of existence those lessons (bitter but indispensable) that bring him to a full appreciation of his divine identity as an eternal individual in relationship with a Parent-God. Hence, for Kierkegaard, true spirituality means *personal* and *passionate* encounter with a *personal* and *passionate* God—a God who is a "subject"

> and therefore exists only for subjectivity in inwardness . . . [R]eflection is directed to the question whether *the individual* is related to a something *in such a manner* that his relationship is in truth a God-relationship. . . . That very instant he has God, not by virtue of any objective deliberation but by virtue of the infinite passion of inwardness. . . . God is precisely that which one takes *a tout prix*, which in the understanding of passion constitutes the true inward relationship to God. (1969, pp. 211–212)

This "God-relationship" begins as a "primitive gripping" of the individual *as* an individual by God. "By relating itself to its own self, and by willing to be itself, the self is grounded transparently in the Power which constituted it" (Kierkegaard, 1969, p. 292). This radical act of the self "willing to be itself" by willing to be "grounded" in the parental God, is *faith*. Faith does not—indeed it cannot—rest on mere logic for it must engage—and in engaging, transfigure—the *whole person*, including his reason. Thus, by seeing oneself as having one's being *through* God and coming to know one's utter insignificance *before* him, there arises a humility that is, paradoxically, the first real step on the road to one's eternal progression toward fully divine status.

Dialectic Spirituality and Dialectic Teaching
Current educational discourse concerns itself even less with dialectically spiritual worldviews than unitively spiritual ones. Hence, out purpose here is not to review the literature of dialectically spiritual pedagogy. Except for the work of that great (and woefully underappreciated) curriculum theorist Duane Huebner—and to a lesser degree Philip Phenix, James McDonald, and Parker Palmer—very little of a systematic nature exists. Rather, we would like to imagine what some of the basic contours of a dialectically spiritual pedagogy might be.

Now, we are wrenchingly aware of the fact that monotheism has all too often been used as an ideological cover and theological vindication to promote and then legitimate some of the most beastly acts and horrific warfare that stain the pages of history. The monotheistic religions have also served as the basis for some of the most wretched uses of education as a highly effective way of colonizing a people—"training" them how to perform their work and "educating" them into doctrines that but reinforce their servitude. All of this is, of course, a matter of historical record.

We, however, wish to focus on the enormous potential for psychological wholeness that a monotheistically informed pedagogy can offer—because of its concern with the dignity and identity of the individual along with its commitment to the sanctity of human relationship. This will vouchsafe us yet another purchase on peace and how to attain it intrapersonally and interpersonally, psychically and socially.

To do thus, we will refer to cues and clues in the work of that towering Jewish theologian Martin Buber as well as two great Protestant theologians—Soren Kierkegaard in the nineteenth century and Paul Tillich in the twentieth. We will also reference some Jewish, Islamic, and Christian scriptures and commentaries.

I, Thou, and the Specificity of Encounter

Martin Buber saw the *I–Thou* relationship as the *sine qua non* of spirituality:

> The extended lines of relation meet in the eternal *Thou*: Every *particular Thou* is a glimpse through to the *eternal Thou*; by means of every *particular Thou*, the primary word addresses the *eternal Thou*. Through the mediation of the *Thou* of all beings, fulfillment, and non-fulfillment, of relations comes to them: The inborn *Thou* is realized in each relation and consummated in none. (1965, p. 59)

Buber thus claimed that an authentic *I–Thou* relationship between a teacher and student may lead them both into a dialogical encounter with God. In *both* unitive and dialectic teaching the teacher and student, entering into ever closer relationship, simultaneously move closer to the divine. However, in dialectic spirituality the purpose of this proximity is not absorption into an ultimately impersonal Ground of Being but rather a personally reaffirming relationship with God as the ultimate *Thou*, an eternal *Person*. Thus, "a curriculum of transcendence [provides] a context for engendering, gestating, expecting, and celebrating the moments of singular awareness and of inner illumination when each person comes into the consciousness of his *inimitable personal being*" (Phenix, 1964, p. 128; emphasis added).

> This "singular awareness" of one's "inimitable personal being" is the firmest foundation for "ethical contemplation" because there is only one kind of ethical contemplation, namely, self-contemplation. Ethics closes immediately about the individual, and demands that he exist ethically; it does not make a parade of millions or of generations of men; it does not take humanity in the lump any more than the police arrest humanity at large. If God knows how many hairs there are on each man's head, the ethical knows how many human beings there are; and its enumeration is not in the interest of a total sum, but for the sake of each individual. The ethical requirement is imposed upon each individual, and when it judges, it judges each individual by himself. (Kierkegaard, 1969, p. 226)

Hence, the "the relation in education [should be] one of pure dialogue" between the teacher and student (Buber, 1985, p. 66). In dialectical spirituality and pedagogy, "pure" and mutually enriching dialogue is not only possible but ultimately significant because each conversant carries within himself a unique seed of divine identity. The pedagogical encounter will necessarily be different in each teacher-student dyad—although they will naturally tend to be similar in many ways, too. Generally, war is characterized by, or at least begins in, a breakdown of dialogue. By teaching what real and robust dialogue is in his class and modeling it for his students in virtually their every interaction with them, the teacher helps mold his students into precisely the kind of people who are less likely to go to war, preferring dialogical contact with the Other, not wishing to obliterate him in countless sieges and counter-sieges of reckless rhetorical bombardment.

In reading the four gospels as well as the other canonical literature in our churches, the authors have always been struck by how Jesus as a teacher and healer responds differently to individuals who have the same problem. For instance, one blind person he heals by simply placing his hands over her eyes; to another, he restores sight by spitting in the dirt and applying a bit of mud; another he heals by the words he speaks to her; another he heals at a distance with a mere thought. Jesus is so supremely present *in* and *as* himself, and *in* and *as* relationship with his Heavenly Father, that he naturally tailors his message and methods to the reality of each specific person with whom he is presently dealing. "How powerful, even to the point of being overbearing," says the Jewish theologian, Buber:

> and how legitimate, even to the point of being self-evident, is the saying of *I* by Jesus. For it is the *I* of unconditional relation in which the man calls his *Thou* Father in such a way that he is simply Son, and nothing else but Son. Whenever he says *I*, he can only mean the *I* of the holy primary word that has been raised for him into unconditional being. If separation ever touches him, his solidarity of relation is the greater; he speaks to others only out of this solidarity. (Buber, 1985, p. 67)

Likewise, the teacher's most important role is to speak to her students "out of this solidarity" with God. This is more important than knowledge of subject-matter, which, although unquestionably significant, is less than ultimately consequential if it is not divinely grounded. This does not mean that the teacher should use religious language or introduce religious concepts, which, unless they are directly relevant to the curriculum, are legally prohibited in U.S. public schools (*Abington et al. v. Schempp et al.*, 374 US 203 [1963]; *Lemon v. Kurtzman*, 403 US 602 [1971]). But it does entail speaking in a manner and with a voice that testifies—implicitly and with ease—to the teacher's personal relationship with that which he considers ultimate.

Such teaching is religious regardless of either the subject-matter or the teacher's formal religious commitments (or lack thereof)—for this teacher recognizes that in his classroom "hovering always is *the absolute 'other,'* Spirit, that overwhelms us in moments of awe, terror, tragedy, beauty, and peace. Content is the 'other.' Knowing is the process of being in relationship with that 'other.' Knowledge is an abstraction from that process" (Huebner, 1999, p. 408). By experiencing the action of the Spirit of God as it discloses the secrets of *any* subject matter, the teacher and student come to an *I-Thou* encounter with that Person who is the fundamental truth behind all contingent ones.

> The curriculum allows personal encounter in another sense as well. For, what the teacher and student are presently examining—a story, say, or an artifact or theory—embodies the comings and goings of other people. In their comings and goings—their journeys and pilgrimages—they house themselves, construct tools and equipment, negotiate institutions, engage and interact with flora and fauna. And when they rest and relax from the struggles of life and have time to contemplate and converse, they tell stories of where they have been and where they are going, they sing and dance and paint and build so they will not forget what they have endured and experienced and hoped for. (Huebner, 1999, p. 362)

Thus trained over the many years of his schooling in attending to both the grandeur as well as the subtleties of other cultures, the student grows into an advocate of intercultural communication and less an agent of one state struggling to bring another to its knees in acts of violence.

Education as Repentance
Another distinguishing feature of dialectical spiritualities is their rather unpopular insistence upon the *reality of sin* and *the need for repentance and atonement*. Only when we acknowledge the sway of sin in our individual and collective lives—sin that we both suffer and perpetrate—can we begin to appreciate the immensity of God's goodness and the miracle of his forgiveness. According to the dialectical religions, such an attitude—stripped of brassy pride—is the first step in becoming "teachable" enough for God to begin to reveal knowledge of things as they *are*—not as we, in our vain and self-serving imaginings, *suppose* that they are or *should* be. The great Islamic poet Rumi therefore taught: "Fear not to acknowledge your ignorance and guilt,/That the Heavenly Master may not withhold instruction" (1975, p. 189).

No matter how vociferously our postmodern world claims to have outgrown the concept of sin as a benighted irrelevancy, both common sense and the news nevertheless convey the daily message that sin is real. For there will always be sin so long as a person or group of people treat another person or group of people as objects to satisfy their own ambitions and lusts. This forms the moral basis in a dialectically spiritual pedagogy of denouncing any attempt to treat teachers or students as economic objects—"human capital," to use that odious term. Despite their unctuous rhetoric of concern for teachers and students, both neoliberal and neoconservative federal "reform" agendas—that is, Reagan's *A Nation at Risk*, Clinton's *Goals 2000*, and Bush's *No Child Left Behind*—would turn teachers and students into cogs in the machine of transnational corporate capitalism.

In dialectical terms, these agendas are sinful. What is more, it is also sinful to treat subject matter as a mere object. Buber lamented: "O accumulation of information! It—always it" (1965, p. 5). T. S. Eliot asked, "Where is the wisdom we have lost in knowledge?/Where is the knowledge we have lost in information?" (1971, p. 96).

History and the Curriculum in Dialectical Spirituality

Monotheistic religions insist that the patterns of human history are neither illusory (as in postmodernism) nor simply repetitive (as in Buddhism and Hinduism). History is linear and has a purpose: the establishment of the Kingdom of God on a transfigured earth. We see this difference between unitive and dialectic spirituality in their teleological metaphors. Unitively viewed, personal and collective history are considered dreams from which we must awaken and detach. Dialectically, however, history is seen as a divine drama with which we must fully engage and identify. The burden of the dialectic curriculum is to help each student understand her world-historical destiny and responsibility as an individual agent in that process—to grasp the fact that "the world is not divine sport, it is divine destiny. There is divine meaning in the life of the world, of man, of human persons, of you and of me" (Buber, 1965, p. 82).

But because we are often wayward as individuals and nations, the God of history must try to get us back on the right path by offering us the chance (if we will only choose to take it!) of listening to the voices of his chosen representatives—his *prophets*. The prophetic "vocation" is very similar across the dialectical religions. "The prophet Mohammed's divine commission is the same that had fallen on Abraham, Moses, Samuel, Isaiah and Jesus. Whenever, wherever this call comes, its form may differ but its message is the same: A voice from Heaven saying, 'Thou art the messenger!'" (Smith, 1958, p. 197). This momentous call, coming to an individual from the ultimate Individual, empowers the prophet, in the unique tenor of his own voice, to call other individuals to personal and social repentance and reformation. The Prophet cries in the Holy Koran, "O my people! Enter the holy land which Allah hath assigned unto you, and turn not back ignominiously, for then will ye be overthrown, to your own ruin" (Surah 5, Al Ma'idah 4: 21). And Micah proclaims, "What doth the Lord require of thee, but to do justly, and to love mercy, and to walk humbly with thy God? The Lord's voice crieth unto the city. . . ." We are God's historical coworkers—a political faith is at the heart of many liberatory theologies and pedagogies (Schipani, 1988).

There is no set formula for the teacher to galvanize the student to this prophetic, world-historical vision—merely the imperative that she do so, encouraging each student to determine for himself his historical situatedness, his roles and responsibilities. Cliff knows a high school teacher who has her students read Howard Zinn's (1990) socialist interpretation of American history in addition to the standard U.S. history text that her district requires. Throughout the term, she asks her students, "How does the official text vary from Zinn's? Which one seems more credible to you, and why? What might account for the differences between the texts? Whose interests are served by buying into one interpretation over the other? And what does all of this imply as to *your* role and responsibility locally, nationally, globally?"

In sum, the teacher-as-prophet, on the strength of his unique experience of a personal, historical God, not only infuses his teaching with that vision but spurs students on to their own encounters and insights. This pedagogical dynamic merely reflects the prophetic infrastructure of education in those many cultures for which encounter between God and their prophets are key. Students memorize the Torah and the Koran. Native American children are taught to commit to heart the oral traditions from the beginning of the earth—the words of those messengers who have come bearing salvific lessons from the Great Father in Heaven. They are also encouraged to have their own vision quest along with a new name symbolizing their own immortal individual identity (Hirschfelder & Molin, 1992). Many indigenous cultures rest upon the prophetic role of the shaman, who is uniquely able to travel to and converse with God, from whom he brings back the oracles of life to the community of the faithful (Eliade, 1974).

For all the insistence upon the reality of sin and the need for repentance, dialectical spirituality and pedagogy radiate historical optimism and thus set the stage for a principled commitment to and faith in the possibility for peace to spread over several generations and change the course of our specie's evolution. Such faith in the God of Peace and that God's actions in history are what keeps hope alive and what therefore keeps the struggle for peace growing. Wrote Tillich in sweeping prose reminiscent of St. Paul:

> The content of faith in Providence is this: when death rains from heaven as it does now, when cruelty wields power over nations and individuals as it does now, when hunger and persecution drive millions from place to place, as they do now, and when prisons and slums all over the world throughout history

> degrade the humanity of the bodies and souls of men as they do now—we can boast in that time, and just in that time, that even all of this cannot separate us from the love of God. In this sense, and in this sense alone, all things work together for good, for the *ultimate* good, the eternal love, and the Kingdom of God. Faith in divine Providence is the faith that nothing can prevent us from fulfilling the ultimate meaning of our existence. Providence does not mean a divine planning by which everything is predetermined as an efficient machine. Rather, Providence means that there is a creative and saving possibility implied in every situation, which cannot be destroyed by any event. Providence means the daemonic and destructive forces within ourselves and our world can never have an unbreakable grasp upon us, and that the bond which connects us with the fulfilling love can never be disrupted. (Tillich, 1976, p. 107)

The ahistorical views of "history" as fiction or repetition pose less of a challenge to the spiritually dialectical view of history than the vaunting assumption that history *has* a purpose—but one that is entirely in the hands of human beings alone. As faith in something that we have made and to which we then ascribe saving power, such approaches are seen as *ideological idolatry*. The capitalist faith in an efficient economy to bring about human fulfillment exemplifies such idolatry as does its philosophical cousin, Marxism.

As is always true of idolatry, ideological idolatry relies on political sleight-of-hand—the attempt to manipulate people *impersonally* through mere techniques and technologies that are not grounded in the individual concern of a loving God for each of His children as a unique being with free will. The curriculum becomes trickery whenever it serves merely political or economic purposes, placing itself at the service of techno-corporate gods. Merely technological or financial goals, although legitimate as secondary aims of education, are catastrophic as its raison d'être.

The dialogical union of the teacher and student is thus a form of political resistance, for it reflects and affirms the fact history is "divine destiny" which, according to many dialectical religions, will consist in loving communion in justice and righteousness between divinely transfigured individuals on a reborn earth, where "old things are passed away; behold, all things are become new" (2 Corinthians 5:17). The teacher who grounds his teaching in this or a similar hope is a prophet and will serve no national or fiscal gods (Bullough, Patterson, & Mayes, 2002). For he knows that "God educates. We don't. But God can educate only if we hearken to [John the Baptist's prophetic] call 'Prepare ye the Way!' We participate in God's educational work by bringing under criticism our self made world, and by proclaiming God's presence. . . . We are but [His] servants" (Huebner 1999, p. 400).

The Certainty of Doubt
Surprisingly perhaps, doubt is a necessary element of prophetic teaching. If Tillich (1959) was right that religion is "ultimate concern" about one's existence, then doubt is highly religious because it is an excruciating *surplus* of concern that cries out for a divine response that does not seem to be forthcoming. Indeed, without doubt, faith would not be faith—but knowledge. The courageous response to doubt is the personal risk of faith in a personal God, who, like any parent or friend, wants us to trust him—and to do so because he is embedded in our hearts, not because he has provided some sort of flashy proof in response to our clamorous cries for "evidence" of his existence and care. Such faith is risky, but what important relationship is not? "Without risk there is no faith, and the greater the risk, the greater the faith; the more objective security, the less inwardness (for inwardness is precisely subjectivity), and the less objective security, the more profound the possible inwardness" (Kierkegaard, 1969, pp. 11–12).

Accordingly, the dialectically spiritual educator does not shy away from heart-felt uncertainties, nor does he gloss over his students' or his own epistemic limitations. He openly acknowledges these things, even welcomes them, wrestling with their complexity both privately in his meditations and publicly with his students.

Indeed, he *requires* himself and his students to explore the critically constructive possibilities of doubt, for it is only in this way that each student can learn for himself how to discover and enact his commitment to God in a manner that is true to his unique relationship with him. The radically dualistic interplay of doubt and faith is, then, at the heart of any dialectical spirituality and pedagogy that hopes to lay claim to existential authenticity. It is also a precondition of peace, for a wide vision among various parties of each other's legitimate point of view may well conclude in détente, not destruction.

Conclusion

This chapter has revealed many similarities between unitively and dialectically spiritual visions of education, the most important one being that both are unabashedly spiritual. This is no small matter in current educational discourse, which is governed, on one side, by technist approaches to education and, on the other side, by the desire to see educational issues almost exclusively in political terms (whether the politics are modernist or postmodernist). Technical and political considerations are important in formulating an educational theory and practicing it in the classroom, of course. However, when primarily spiritual approaches are marginalized, as is now manifestly the case, then there is reason to celebrate the courage and vision of both unitive and dialectical theorists and practitioners, who champion the spiritual point-of-view; for, it is these two forms of spirituality which—each in its own way—are capable of promoting peace through educational means.

This is all the more true when we realize that such approaches to education provide uniquely powerful bases for resisting the encroachment of corporate capitalism into our classrooms, which should be havens for loving encounter, not training grounds for economic functionaries. Both spiritual pedagogies offer powerful ideas and practices for protecting, even enshrining, the sanctity of the teacher-student relationship, ascribing to teachers the dignity they richly merit but would be hard-pressed to find to such a degree and with such an intensity in other pedagogies. This is evidenced in the image of the teacher as a Zen master or a prophet. Clearly, there are many reasons that unitively and dialectically spiritual pedagogies should join hands in advancing the holistic goal of spiritualizing educational systems that are so stubbornly resistant to transcendent perspectives.

We would not wish, of course, to minimize the very real differences between these two spiritualities and pedagogies. Even here, however, there are wonderful possibilities for pedagogical cross-fertilization.

A dialectically spiritual pedagogy has a great deal to learn from the unitively spiritual pedagogies, which shine in their profound reverence for nature, their insistence upon gender and cultural sensitivity, their compassionate attunement to the needs and possibilities of aging, and their ancient traditions and manifold techniques of honoring and integrating all aspects of the student's being. Dialectically spiritual approaches to education also have much to offer. Stemming from a venerable and complexly articulated tradition of world-historical vision, they provide grounding and direction to the politics of the spirit in teaching.

They also provide a vision of the student as a unique being whose identity is particularly precious because it is eternally consequential and durable. For both younger students, who are involved in the process of identity formation, and older ones, who are facing with special poignancy the fact of their own mortality, dialectically spiritual pedagogies proffer a unique brand of hope regarding personal and interpersonal reality on the other side of this mortal veil.

In other words, each of these two visions should represent one side of the precious coin of spirituality in education, which, alone, can help us purchase peace both within and among individuals.

CHAPTER THREE

Psychological Wholeness
The Precondition for Peace

As we discussed in the previous chapter, the more whole one is psychologically, the more one experiences life through balanced or centered thinking. Such a mind has mastered a vast array of psychological tools making equanimity and peace more attainable—even when great challenges arise. Wholeness from a psychological standpoint is essential if humanity expects to be capable of choosing peace. Peace comes from the ability to assess situations accurately, meet circumstances with balanced thinking, act with awareness, and feel empathetic concern for the other party. Peace cannot be forced through laws, although laws are important in establishing and maintaining a modicum of civility. True peace develops through a state of elevated consciousness.

Psychological wholeness allows one to see more accurately, not to be caught as often by the blaming, shameful, defensive, threatened, or fearful thinking that so often colors our interpretations. As one becomes more centered, one begins to relate to the world more wholeheartedly and with more empathy and compassion, being able to interpret challenging situations less personally, with more security, keeping the threatened, fearful responses at bay more of the time.

It is common to struggle psychologically, for that is the way the personality grows into a more emotionally mature mind. Yet, many do not learn the tools, and they repeat the same patterns at various times through the course of their life. An example of this would be the person who seems to get fired every few years because her supervisor "always stifles her creativity," or the man who is repeatedly "backed into a corner" by the overbearing woman he chooses to be in relationship with, who turns out to be just like his mother. Repeating a pattern signals lack of growth, since no new strategies are investigated and no new neural pathways learn to fire. The person does not possess enough new information to create opportunities for different, more favorable outcomes; the context changes, but the ego consciousness travels round and round like on a hamster wheel. New strategies require different thinking. It is easier to point the finger at those outside himself who seem to be "at fault," without evaluating his own responsibility in the exchange. It is painful to see through the ego's veil; the ego ardently defends one's default way of thinking.

A study conducted by Ronald Kessler, professor at Harvard Medical School, who received the Senior Scientist and MERIT awards for excellent research from the National Institute of Mental Health, looks at psychiatric disorders that are prevalent in a probability sample of civilians in the United States between fifteen to fifty-four years of age: "Nearly 50% of respondents reported at least one lifetime disorder, and close to 30% reported at least one 12-month disorder. . . . Less than 40% of those with a lifetime disorder had ever received professional treatment" (Kessler et al., 1994). These statistics are staggering.

Kessler and team conclude, "The prevalence of psychiatric disorders is greater than previously thought to be the case. Furthermore, this morbidity is more highly concentrated than previously recognized in roughly one-sixth of the population who have a history of three or more comorbid [occurring together] disorders" (*Lifetime and 12-Month Prevalence of DSM-III-R Psychiatric Disorders in the United States*, 8).

Kessler and team found that one sixth of the population have a history of three or more disorders and half the population has at least one disorder. Kessler continues, "The majority of people with psychiatric disorders fail to obtain professional treatment. Even among people with a lifetime history of three or more comorbid disorders, the proportion who ever obtain specialty sector mental health treatment is less than 50%. These results argue for the importance of more outreach and more research on barriers to professional help-seeking" (Kessler et al., 1994). Why do so few who suffer from psychological disorders seek help? Kessler states, "The majority of those who received no treatment felt that they did not have an emotional problem requiring treatment" (Kessler et al., 2001, p. 987).

Dysfunctional thinking hides beneath the onslaught of emotions; to the thinker these emotions and mental structures are her usual pattern for relating. Therefore, they feel normal to her mind. She does not see a scale or an example of what effective thinking looks and feels like compared with her own unless she seeks help psychologically, and the research shows that to be improbable. As Kessler suggests, would awareness of what mental health looks and acts like create more willingness to seek help?

While many scales exist to compare one's thinking to that of a healthy mind, such as the Taylor-Johnson Temperament Analysis, which measures eighteen dimensions of personality that are important elements of personal adjustment and effective interpersonal relationships, they are not easily accessible to the general population.

What the Schools Can Do to Promote Mental Health

We looked previously in some depth at the attempt—largely unsuccessful—to make achieving and maintaining mental health a central goal or education in the United States. We have learned a great deal over the last century about what works and does not work clinically in promoting mental health in the schools as well as about the political resistance such a movement encounters and how to overcome it. If only we can muster the courage and instill the vision in parents, educators, and school and district leaders that insists upon making self-awareness, emotional self-regulation, and the cultivation of compassion primary goals of education, it seems highly probable that we can effect a seachange in the general mental health of our citizenry.

To take just one example, what if we made psychological testing a part of the education system. This would give students the opportunity, if they and their parents saw fit, to process and act upon the valuable insights revealed by the tests so that the children and parents might learn to take more responsibility for what they bring to their relationships and what they manifest in their lives—especially, perhaps, in school settings.

Daniel Goleman, author of *Emotional Intelligence*, weighs in on this question as follows: "By leaving the emotional lessons children learn to chance, we risk largely wasting the window of opportunity presented by the slow maturation of the brain to help children cultivate a healthy emotional repertoire" (1995, p. 286). Awareness sets the stage for psychological wellness to be a part of their internal conversation. This type of education would bring to mind throughout life the importance of nurturing psychological and spiritual well-being just as we nurture the physical body through exercise and eating well. This kind of knowledge, combined with practice in meditation throughout the school years, from K through 12, would give our students untold advantages that their predecessors never had in self-knowledge and self-regulation.

The Nueva Learning Center near San Francisco is a school educating students from pre-kindergarten through twelfth grade. The curriculum includes social-emotional learning (previously called self-science), age appropriate for each year, and principles of neuroscience that encourage effective communications. This program strives to teach self-awareness, self-management, social awareness which includes relating with empathy, relationship skills, and responsible decision making.

As explained by Goleman, "The topics taught include self-awareness, in the sense of recognizing feelings and building a vocabulary for them, and seeing the links between thoughts, feelings, and reactions; knowing if thoughts or feelings are ruling a decision; seeing the consequences of alternative choices; and applying these insights to decisions about such issues as drugs, smoking, and sex" (1995, 268). These tools are fundamental mechanics for a well-lived life, yet so many do not have these tools in their psychological toolbox.

Goleman goes on to say, "Another emphasis is managing emotions: realizing what is behind a feeling, and learning ways to handle anxieties, anger and sadness. Still another emphasis is on taking responsibility for decisions and actions and following through on commitments. A key social ability is empathy, understanding others' feelings and taking their perspective, and respecting differences in how people feel about things" (p. 268).

These children are being taught to more effectively meet the world as an adolescent, teenager, and adult. They are learning tools that will help in their careers and their relationships including marriage and connection with their own children. "Although such courses do not change anyone over night, as children advance through the curriculum from grade to grade, there are discernible improvements in the tone of a school and the outlook—and the level of emotional competence—of the girls and boys who take them" (Goleman 1995, p. 283). How might the United States change in fifty years if every school had such a curriculum? What would the impact be on the world at large if every school in the world participated in a similar curriculum? Whatever it would be, it is simply peevish and cynical to think it would do anything less than good . . . and perhaps enormous good.

The inner journey of learning who we are is for everyone, not just for the 50 percent of us who suffer from mental illness at some point in our lives. It is not about prescribing a formula for every student to follow. It is also not about testing, categorizing, shaming, or separating out those who are more challenged emotionally. It is the process of showing humanity a picture of mental health and providing opportunity for everyone to evolve and explore her own well-being. The student cannot be forced to take the journey to self-knowledge. The student must find inspiration from within—to cherish who she is and impart her light to shine brightly. If she does not see this, it is not her time but at least the seeds of awareness have been planted.

As mentioned earlier, the ego will do everything in its power to maintain the status quo, no matter how chaotic the status quo is. The ego has an ingenious denial system designed to keep mental illness from being seen by the conscious mind. Dysfunctional thinking is laced with paranoia, defensiveness, anger, hostility, fear, rage, mistrust, and more. If roughly 50 percent of the population experience life through such dysfunctional filters, at least some of the time, it will not be possible to create a world where compassion and empathy are a priority. Everything depends upon significantly reducing this number.

The inner journey is a painstaking process and not a journey to be taken lightly. This journey is our inner calling, pleading with us to find our best self, buried deep within; it is the call to begin our hero's journey. As Joseph Campbell reminds us, "Each in his lifetime is in the process of bringing forth a specimen of humanity such as never before was made visible upon this earth, and the way to this achievement is not along anyone else's path who ever lived" (2007, p. 226).

This journey addresses the emptiness that presents itself after the achievement you have sought so diligently to attain. It addresses those who function well in society but find some limits to their ability to find peace, happiness, and joy. This call to action seeks those who find life not as fulfilling as they hoped, those who suffer from acute and severe depression, those who are unconscious to how their behavior affects others, those who are caught by anger, rage, and impatience, those who find it difficult to work with others, those who do not relate easily with empathy and compassion, those who do not understand how to listen, those who do not know how to encourage. The call also reaches those who are threatened by the success of others, those who are afraid of their own light, those who shame and blame others, those who believe they are worthless and incapable of greatness. This arduous adventure beckons every human being. This journey is the journey of becoming who you are. How do we work toward becoming whole?

Individuation and Emotional Intelligence

Carl Jung describes the inner journey as the individuation process. Jung explains, "I use the term 'individuation' to denote the process by which a person becomes a psychological 'in-dividual,' that is, a separate indivisible unity or 'whole'" (1951/1968, para. 490). This journey to wholeness is attained through self-knowledge. In analysis one is prompted and guided as she first uncovers her complexes and then begins to look into her shadow and uncover parts of her unconscious motivations, which in time will change how she relates to and sees the world. As more awareness is brought to these unconscious motivations, the more balanced and unified her psyche becomes. Without the depth of looking into the unconscious or the shadow, without balancing the two forces of conscious and unconscious, light and dark, psychotherapy does not reach its potential. Jung states, "This rounding out of the personality into a whole may well be the goal of any psychotherapy that claims to be more than a mere cure of symptoms" (1951/1968, para. 524). The individuation process is more than a cure for symptoms; it is diving into the mysterious abyss of her psyche to learn who she is.

The more unconscious or fragmented one's psyche/spirit, the more one will struggle to see beyond the ego's narrow perspective. The individuation process challenges our standard way of thinking; it is a journey where the conscious and unconscious establish relations. The journey is prompted by the unavoidable challenge of facing one's inner dragons that live in the oblivion of the unconscious mind and seem to scorch one's fear and pain with fire-breathing rage. It takes courage to look at the darkness, to see the parts of oneself that are dreadful. Jung explains, "Western man confronts himself as a stranger and that self-knowledge is one of the most difficult and exacting of the arts" (1955–1956/1970a, para. 709).

Learning to honor all aspects of who one is, with balance—the light and the dark—is the process of becoming whole. This is a result of fervently seeking consciousness and self-knowledge. Jung points out, "We could therefore translate individuation as 'coming to selfhood' or 'self-realization'" (1953, para. 266). Self-realization is unraveling the psyche by looking into one's default ways of thinking and becoming conscious of the reactions that seem automatic and that breed limited views and inaccurate thinking. It is learning how to find a necessary distance from the feelings of discomfort and the eruption of emotion that usually follows. In this distance from the feelings of discomfort and the need to react, there is space for a conscious decision along much healthier psychological and ethical lines to be made.

As one embarks on the individuation process, she is first called to look at her complexes that color her perceptions. Complexes include ineffective thinking that blind the person from seeing beyond her personal "insider" perspective. Complexes create reactivity and are commonly laced with fear, anger, blame, or defensiveness. Jung teaches that:

> The more "complexes" a man has, the more he is possessed. . . . But if such a man makes himself conscious of his unconscious contents, as they appear firstly in the factual contents of his personal unconscious, and then in the fantasies of the col-

lective unconscious, he will get to the roots of his complexes, and in this way rid himself of his possession. (1953, para. 387)

Complexes feel like default settings—preset, automated responses, as Jung characterizes it, "factual contents." The more possessed by one's complexes and projections, the more rigid one's beliefs. Said the Buddha of rigidity, "Thinking we already possess the truth, we will be unable to open our minds to receive the truth, even if truth comes knocking at our door" (Hanh, 1991, p. 212). The information filtered through a complex seems like it is the only possible "correct" information, and that excessive passion and judgment are the only possible responses to a situation that presses all the individual's buttons

For example, one with a superiority complex filters information about the world through the inner perception that she is better and more competent than others. She is the one who takes the knife out of your hand as you slice the onion, under the guise of teaching a better way to cut the onion. One who has an inferiority complex filters information through the inner perception that she is less than and less competent than others. She is the one who is usually uncomfortable making decisions and often says, "I do not know; what do you think?" She is quick to give up responsibility to another party as she feels they are more competent. The countless different complexes touch the interpretation of every experience in one's life, and the more unconscious she is of her complexes, the more she will be possessed by its filters.

As the complexes become more conscious and one gains tools to see through these marred lenses, she begins to look into the shadow and make conscious parts of her psyche that are denied or repressed. Jung wrote, "The shadow personifies everything that the subject refuses to acknowledge about himself and yet is always thrusting itself up on him directly or indirectly—for instance, inferior traits of character and other incompatible tendencies" (1951/1968, para. 513). The shadow is thrusting itself up looking for voice, as the subject ignores its call and pushes away. The subject, unable to recognize these inferior traits in herself, experiences them through projection and self-sabotaging behaviors, all of which are unconscious. Jung elaborates:

> The shadow is a moral problem that challenges the whole ego-personality, for no one can become conscious of the shadow without considerable moral effort. To become conscious of it involves recognizing the dark aspects of the personality as present and real. This act is the essential condition for any kind of self-knowledge, and it therefore, as a rule, meets with considerable resistance. Indeed, self-knowledge as a psychotherapeutic measure frequently requires much painstaking work extending over a long period. (1951/1968, para. 14)

The seeker is called to endure much toil and unavoidable pain on the road to self-knowledge and therefore it is not a popular road to travel. "Jung believed that only exceptional individuals reached the peaks of individual development" (Jung, 1983, p. 20).

The ego has the limited perspective of the tip of an iceberg, where the unconscious is the enormous mass below. When the unconscious is not a part of the conversation, the ego believes it is the sole leader despite the surging unconscious. The more rigid and dogmatic the ego is at hiding its shadow side, the more monstrous the expression of the suppressed unconscious will become. Jung goes on to assert, "If we understand anything of the unconscious, we know that it cannot be swallowed. We also know that it is dangerous to suppress it, because the unconscious is life and this life turns against us if suppressed, as happens in neurosis" (1951/1968, para. 521). This is where self-sabotaging behaviors step in.

When the unconscious begins to become a part of one's awareness, the personality is mindful to some degree of the underlying psyche needs that may wish to emerge from the shadows. This personality is not jailed in a psychological prison of ignorance because she allows expression of the shadow; self-knowledge enables the shadow to find its proper voice. She does not fear the shadow, she explores it with curiosity. It is a constant unveiling. "This is what I mean by the individuation process. As the name shows, it is a process or course of development arising out of the conflict between the two fundamental psychic facts [the conscious and the unconscious]" (1951/1968, para. 523).

As the conscious and unconscious become balanced, allowing both sides a voice, the ego is no longer the dictator. "Conscious and unconscious do not make a whole when one of them is suppressed and injured by the other. If they must contend, let it at least be a fair fight with equal rights on both sides. Both are aspects of life. Consciousness should defend its reason and protect itself, and the chaotic life of the unconscious should be given the chance of having its way too. . . . It is the old game of hammer and anvil: between them the patient iron is forged into an indestructible whole, an 'individual'" (1951/1968, para. 522).

Awareness begins to slowly filter through unconscious thinking patterns. This does not mean there are no longer blind spots; it means one has learned to question the darkness and her interpretations of the feelings behind her automatic reactions. A wider, bigger, more whole perspective emerges which incorporates light and dark, yin and yang. The opposites, when balanced, complement each other because they exist in harmony—there is no longer a fight between them. This is the journey toward wholeness.

Through self-knowledge, one unifies the polarities of light and dark. In *Wisdom of Imperfection*, therapist and Buddhist Rob Preece has written that "individuation implies becoming ever more conscious of, and fully open to, all that we are, be it good or bad, so as to become increasingly whole" (2006, p. 11). The individuation process uncovers this place of paradox and gives rise to self-compassion which allows both sides to exist in balance—to see the fallibility in one's humanity. Being vulnerable to the rest of humanity while holding that fallibility creates authenticity and connection to the rest of the world.

It is very difficult as conditioned westerners to give our darkness a voice. It is so much easier to push it away in fear, deny its existence. One of the telling dichotomies in our culture is portrayed in the Christian mythos; Christ is all good, Satan is all bad. This motif separates good and evil into two different beings.

This opposition is a powerful stimulus for repression and projection of the darkness within. There is no way to rid oneself of her darkness—that is suppression. Jung goes on to say, "So far as we can judge from experience, light and shadow are so evenly distributed in man's nature that his psychic totality appears, to say the least of it, in a somewhat murky light" (1951/1968, para. 76). We are all made up of light and dark, we are murky—yet that which we feed will grow, that which we allow a voice will be at ease because it is heard.

One may strive to be solely Christ-like, but in time the shadow will find a way to voice its existence; the more deeply hidden in the unconscious, the more extreme or impudent the voice of her shadow may be. That which is repressed or denied will find voice, like a caged lion recklessly clawing its way to freedom. Yet when the seeker finds a way to hold the Christ-like part in a loving embrace with the darker element, she will have found balance in the self. The vulnerability of seeing and expressing the existence of one's darkness releases the fear attached to this darkness, which tears away its hold on one's psyche.

In order to see through one's neuroses, a person must take responsibility for everything that is manifesting in her life. Both the victim and the bully must take responsibility for their part in the dysfunctional dance they choose—as every other neurotic manifestation. Thinking from a victim point of view looks something like, "I cannot believe this is happening to me. My boss is so unfair. I always attract cruel men." Like all neuroses there are varying degrees of dysfunction with the extreme victim being trapped in the addictive cycle of the emotionally and physically abusive relationship. Taking responsibility does not mean that one holds all the blame or fault. It is a process of seeing one's part in the struggle and seeing the possibility of thinking differently to create a more favorable outcome.

There is no way to be whole psychologically and stay in an abusive relationship. There is no way to manifest one's highest self and remain in a painful relationship. Pain does not mean challenge; all relationships will entail challenges. Rather, it means that one must grow out of relationships that act as psychological handcuffs; one must change her thinking so that she is no longer tolerant with people who minimize, abuse, shame, bully, or otherwise psychologically harm her. Likewise, she must not fall into bullying, abusing, shaming, or psychologically harming others. Peace is impossible when neurotic thinking is the primary way of relating to the world. Jung asks, "How can anyone see straight when he does not even see himself and that darkness which he himself carries unconsciously into all his dealings?" (1940/1969, p. 102).

A victim seeks a bully or an abuser, just as a bully seeks a victim; responsibility comes when both sides see their part in the dysfunctional cycle. Peace comes when people are sufficiently whole and self-checks arise quickly when that wholeness is being threatened. The simplicity of this explanation does not adequately reflect the courage and determination it takes to change one's thinking.

Projection is another part of the denial process. It creates the misperception that those outside of her are wrong, bad, annoying, impatient, or any other cast-out emotion when, in reality, it is inside oneself. "I (the projector) identify with something in you and then I can complain about it without having to look into or evaluate myself" (Ciaramicoli & Ketcham, 2000, p. 104). Projection impedes self-knowledge because the focus is out there. Self-knowledge is looking at what is happening inside one's body, mind, and spirit—to the point where what is happening out there in the external world means less. Jung reminds us that "all projections are unconscious identifications with the object. Every projection is simply there as an uncriticized datum of experience, and is recognized for what it is only very much later, if ever" (1955–1956/1970a, para. 696).

Projection is a tool used by the ego to hide that which it does not wish to see, and they are difficult to see through because they feel factual. "The psychological rule says that when an inner situation is not made conscious, it happens outside, as fate" (1951/1968, p. 126).

Writes von Franz, "Although all the contents of the unconscious are in this fashion projected onto the environment, we can recognize them as projections only when we gain enough insight to see that they are images of peculiarities that are part of our own makeup; otherwise we are naively convinced that these peculiarities belong to the object" (1978/1980, p. 6). The ego with its cunning persuasion absolutely resists the emergence of consciousness. Projections lay hidden; Thus, Jung concludes that "no matter how obvious it may be to the neutral observer that it is a matter of projections, there is little hope that the subject will perceive this himself" (1951/1968, para. 16).

Jung profoundly observes:

> It is often tragic to see how blatantly a man bungles his own life and the lives of others yet remains totally incapable of seeing how much the whole tragedy originates in himself, and how he continually feeds it and keeps it going. Not *consciously*, of course—for consciously he is engaged in bewailing and cursing a faithless world that recedes further and further into the distance. Rather, it is an unconscious factor which spins the illusions that veil his world. And what is being spun is a cocoon, which in the end will completely envelop him. (*1951/1968*, para. 18)

If we actually saw these behaviors in our own being, instead of projecting them on our neighbors, we would have to do something about it—we would have to admit our shortcomings. Jung goes on to say, "Projections can be withdrawn only when they come within the possible scope of consciousness" (1955-1956/1970a, para. 697).

Marc Barasch describes an all-too-common example of projection which mirrors many situations that have created grave unrest:

> In a poll taken in Kosovo in 1997, two years before the genocidal "ethnic cleansing," Serbs and Albanians living in that province were asked to choose which words they thought most accurately described themselves and each other as a group. When it came to themselves, the Albanians selected adjectives like "hospitable, peaceful, courageous, clean, honest, intelligent, united, and hard-working." The Serbs characterized themselves nearly identically. But Serbs described Albanians as "united, those who hate other nations, treacherous, backward, rough, hard-working, exclusive of other nations, and selfish." And, predictably, the Albanians chose virtually the same words to describe the Serbs. With ghastly consequences, both groups lay claim to laudable traits for their own identities while threatening traits are projected outward. (2009, p. 230)

Both groups are engaging in projection, seeing their shadow projected onto the other, making their brand of goodness superior and righteous. It is easy to be blindsided by projection. Gaining consciousness does not mean one is conscious of every projection but that one has sufficient insight to question her motives.

The individuation process tames the ego, eliminating or minimizing greatly the possessive states of emotion that hinder one's ability to see past the illusion of separateness. The dark and the light are both a part of every human being; with such understanding one offers voice to each side, creating balance—harmony between opposites. As mentioned earlier, the child born of Aphrodite and Ares is Harmonia. Balance between the opposing forces of love and war nurtures harmony—compassion and understanding, bringing forth empathy as one learns to see the unwanted aspects of someone else's psyche as a similar vice of their own.

When we are able to see that the evil in another is a potential in our own being, compassion arises. It is not that we embrace bad behavior or hope for darkness, but we learn to honor the journey of pain and sorrow, to see the season of despair and darkness as the place where wisdom is born. Ladner notes that "compassion evokes in us a vision of others and of the environment itself as precious and even as sacred" (2004, p.268). There is a deep caring, a softness that forgives easily, and an ease in the way one relates to that which is sacred.

> When you see the environment as sacred, you become less interested in using it for selfish motives and more interested in preserving it, beautifying it, and relating to it as a means of awakening the best in yourself and others. And when you view yourself and others as sacred, then you naturally see beyond any temporary limitations and negativities to each person's underlying vast potential. (Ladner, 2004, p. 269)

The individuation process is a lifelong journey; as one gains awareness, the process becomes a spiritual endeavor. Jung says, "The more we become conscious of ourselves through self-knowledge, and act accordingly, the more the layer of the personal unconscious that is superimposed on the collective unconscious will be diminished. In this way there arises a consciousness which is no longer imprisoned in the petty, oversensitive, personal world of the ego, but participates freely in the wider world of objective interests" (1953, para. 275). As one becomes more mature in the individuation process, she begins relating on a deeper level to the world, she is not caught by petty differences or insignificant ego-based spats. A person's reactions and responses become more accurate, more empathetic as she learns to honor both her experience and that of the other. She learns to value the experience of the other rather than be threatened or moved to indifference because it is dissimilar to her experience.

At the point where one feels some resolve from her harbored trauma, meditation catapults her to the next incarnation of self-understanding; meditation expounds the limits to one's experience of self-knowledge. "Individuation is essentially a spiritual journey" (Jung, 1983, p. 19). Meditation and the psychology of Buddhism are essentially the teaching of self-knowledge. Through the melding of these two traditions, one gains numerous tools enabling steadfast resilience, bouncing back much more quickly from adversity, and finding new and creative ways to solve challenges and meet heartache. Jung concurs with this:

> Meditation or critical introspection and objective investigation of the object are needed in order to establish the existence of projections. If the individual is to take stock of himself it is essential that his projections should be recognized, because they falsify the nature of the object and besides this contain items which belong to his own personality and should be integrated with it. This is one of the most important phases in the wearisome process of self-knowledge. (1955–1956/1970a, CW 14, para. 710)

The Psychology of Buddhism Expands the Individuation Process

The principles of Buddhist psychology exponentially increase self-awareness, self-acceptance, and self-knowledge. Depth psychology and the psychology of Buddhism work well together, for individuation without meditation may be limiting one's potential to connect with the unified field of oneness, and the teachings of Buddhist psychology without the inner workings of the individuation process may not tend adequately to laying the foundation needed to work through repressed pain and fears. Preece writes, "To resolve deep wounds from abusive relationships, we will often need more than a process of meditation. We may require a period of skillful psychotherapeutic support to enable a gradual release and resolution of trauma" (2006, p. 55).

There is no end to the depths we carry—self-knowledge is a lifelong responsibility. Jung attests that "self-knowledge is an adventure that carries us unexpectedly far and deep" (1955–1956/1970a, CW 14, para. 741). The psychology of Buddhism teaches the foundation for meditation and expanded strategies for gaining more profound freedom from toxic thinking. As explained by Jeffrey Rubin, in *Psychotherapy and Buddhism*, "Psychoanalysis and

Buddhism each have something rare and vital to contribute to the difficulties and challenges of living in our world. The capacity of these two wisdom traditions to help us live with greater self-awareness, self-acceptance, care, and freedom is essential in a world permeated by self-blindness, self-hatred, powerlessness, insensitivity, and alienation" (1996, p. vii).

These two wisdoms work symbiotically to enhance even-mindedness, each deepening different and essential aspects of our self-understanding. Jack Kornfield explains, "The gift of Buddhist psychology is to take us to the next step, the evolutionary capacity to see beyond the separate self" (2008, p. 66). The separate self is another way to describe ego consciousness; the belief that one is separated from the rest of existence—as separate from the whole.

As discussed in the previous chapter, the developments discovered through neuroscience point to many significant improvements to the mind, body, and spirit through regular meditation. Buddhist psychology teaches meditation alongside mindful thinking which encourages self-awareness and self-knowledge. Meditation teaches one to let her emotional state unfold as it may: watching, observing, and understanding that this current emotional state will pass. Meditation slows down emotional reactions, creating a distance from the knee jerk responses. This makes time for the practitioner to choose a different, more effective response. As these emotions rise and fall more consciously, the practitioner gains the ability to manifest different outcomes as her reactions become less habituated and more mindful. "The intention of meditation is to gradually cultivate a quality of presence that is clear and open. . . . With experience, the mind becomes gradually more relaxed yet alert and able to remain in a state of clarity and presence that is no longer disturbed by the arising of appearances, thoughts, or feelings" (Preece, 2006, p. 272). In other words, the mind remains in a state of clarity no matter the circumstances.

The psychology of Buddhism is a method that teaches its student to question her thinking; to see it as an experience that is real but not concrete or factual. It is the experience of the present moment—the judgment of good or bad does not serve her well. The current feelings will pass, the current experience will change. Seeking to hurry past this moment loses its lesson and misses its magic.

The psychology of Buddhism teaches us to honor the emotions that arise, by seeing them for what they are and not being attached, or addicted, to the exhilaration of the emotion or a specific desired outcome. Kornfield clarifies, "Buddhist psychology helps us work with thoughts in two important ways. First, it teaches us how to acknowledge the content of our thoughts. Second, we learn the ability to disentangle from them" (2008, p. 141). In other words, we learn to watch our thoughts rise and fall, without being caught by the need to control or force an outcome.

Buddhist psychology teaches its practitioner to diminish suffering by becoming conscious of ignorance. Kornfield explains, "Buddhist psychology insists we come to terms with the power of our unconscious drives and instincts and the enormous suffering they can cause" (2008, p. 162). Suffering is understood to be created by one's thinking whereas pain is a part of existing in the world; as one walks through seasons of inevitable pain and becomes more conscious of her ignorance, she will begin to face that pain with more equanimity and suffer less. The Buddha declared:

> The case of suffering is ignorance, a false way of looking at reality. Thinking the impermanent is permanent, that is ignorance. Thinking there is a self when there is not, that is ignorance. From ignorance is born greed, anger, fear, jealousy, and countless other sufferings. The path of liberation is the path of looking deeply at things in order to truly realize the nature of impermanence, the absence of a separate self, and the interdependence of all things. This path is the path which overcomes ignorance. Once ignorance is overcome, suffering is transcended. That is true liberation. (in Hanh, 1991, p. 175)

As one begins to see her ignorance or inaccurate understanding, her grip to whatever emotional charge she feels loosens, her vision allows a greater understanding beyond the immediate and small view of emotional crisis, which previously felt like an absolute reality. The Buddha goes on to say, "When we learn to calm our minds in order to look deeply at the true nature of things, we can arrive at full understanding which dissolves every sorrow and anxiety and gives rise to acceptance and love" (in Hanh, 1991, p. 120). This is inner peace.

As consciousness arises, suffering becomes more malleable, and the wisdom gained through one's suffering is realized more quickly. Thich Nhat Hanh describes:

> When you can see the source of your feelings, you will understand their nature. You will see that feelings are impermanent, and gradually you will remain undisturbed by their arising and passing away. Almost all painful feelings have their source in an incorrect way of looking at reality. When you uproot erroneous views, suffering ceases. Erroneous views cause people to consider the impermanent to be permanent. (1991, p. 214)

Understanding that all things change honors the present moment, for the goal is not to keep things as they are but to enjoy them while they are present. This also expands compassion, empathy, and love.

Mindfulness is a tool that deepens one's process of individuation, diving into the depths of our own darkness and simply naming it without judgment—just curiosity. One's inner voice may experience something like, "I am jealous of my colleague who is experiencing great success. I feel like a failure." Mark Epstein explains in his book *Psychotherapy without the Self*, "The practice of mindfulness leads ultimately to a confrontation with the most highly cherished images of the self, a confrontation that is much more likely to be terrifying than oceanic" (2007, p. 134). Confronting the most highly cherished images of one's self is calling everything inside what it is, no games, no masks, no longer able to hide behind one's pretensions. It can be distressing to acknowledge who we really are.

Thich Nhat Hanh insists that "one must look deeply at things in order to penetrate their true nature" (1991, p. 214). The individuation process paves the way for the psychology of Buddhism to realize a deeper letting go of unhealthy attachments—giving rise to more accurate understanding. The more accurate one's understanding, the deeper and richer her life will become as she sees and lives from her true nature beneath layers of suffering.

In the story of the Golden Buddha between the thirteenth and fifteenth century a majestic ten-foot-tall, solid gold Buddha stood, venerated by its community. When the city was under attack, the monks covered the Golden Buddha with clay to conceal its value. The invaders paid no mind to the enormous, worthless statue made of clay. Those who knew of the statue's true nature perished.

Two centuries later the statue was moved to a temple in Bangkok, its true nature still hidden to those who looked upon its rather shoddy exterior. It is said that a monk dreamt the statue was divinely inspired. During the move one of the ropes is said to have broken and the Buddha slipped from the crane, cracking portions of the clay. The monk who dreamt of the divine inspiration saw a shimmer of gold through a crack on the clay-covered statue. He slowly and gently chiseled away the clay, finally revealing the solid gold Buddha which lay beneath. Each of us has a solid gold Buddha nature; we must chip away the clay to reveal our golden Buddha nature beneath. Jack Kornfield expounds, "The primary aim of Buddhist psychology is to help us see beneath this armoring and bring out our original goodness, called our Buddha nature" (2008, p. 12).

There are many layers to the circumstances before us, several which are not initially visible. The psychology of Buddhism teaches its student to open her mind to possibilities beyond her present consciousness and seek understanding outside of her default thinking patterns. This profound awareness is the cornerstone to connection, compassion, and love. One cannot see if one does not understand. One cannot understand if one does not see accurately. Thinking one possesses all the answers is not being open, that is not an attitude which seeks understanding. Thich Nhat Hanh explains:

> Understanding gives rise to compassion and love, which in turn give rise to correct action. In order to love, it is first necessary to understand, so understanding is the key to liberation. In order to attain clear understanding, it is necessary to live mindfully, making direct contact with life in the present moment, truly seeing what is taking place within and outside of oneself. Practicing mindfulness strengthens the ability to look deeply, and when we look deeply into the heart of anything it will reveal itself. This is the secret treasure of mindfulness—it leads to the realization of liberation and enlightenment. (1991, pp. 120–121)

Practicing mindfulness strengthens our ability to look deeply—not only into our own psyche but also into the experience of another. It is difficult to truly see from another person's perspective; one's own experience is so furtively present in all of her thoughts. Susan Bordo explains how we are so inside our own perception that it is difficult to see the blind spots that exist being immersed in that vantage point. The perception is hard to identify because it is always present. She asserts in *The Flight to Objectivity*, "We need to put ourselves 'inside' the experience of others to understand how they 'see' the world. Once inside, we will be forced to recognize just how deeply 'inside' our own experience we always and finally are" (1987, p. 41). One must sincerely part company with the separate self or ego-based thinking to be able to move beyond one's own self-centered perceptions.

Stephen Covey, author of *7 Habits of Highly Successful People*, explains this with a powerful illustration. One Sunday afternoon, Covey was on the subway in New York City. The train was filled with people who were reading, sitting quietly, some lost in thought or resting with eyes closed:

> It was a calm peaceful scene. Then suddenly a man and his children enter the car. The children were so loud and rambunctious that instantly the whole climate changed. The man sat down next to me and closed his eyes, apparently oblivious to the situation. The children were yelling back and forth, throwing things, even grabbing people's papers. It was very disturbing. And yet, the man sitting next to me did nothing. It was difficult not to feel irritated. I could not believe that he could be so insensitive and let his

children run wild like that and do nothing about it, taking no responsibility at all. It was easy to see that everyone on the subway felt irritated, too. So finally, with what I felt was unusual patience and restraint, I turned to him and said, "Sir, your children are really disturbing a lot of people. I wonder if you couldn't control them a little more?" The man lifted his gaze as if to come into consciousness of the situation for the first time and said softly, "Oh, you're right. I guess I should do something about it. We just came from the hospital where their mother died about an hour ago. I don't know what to think. I guess I don't know how to handle it either." (1989/2004, pp. 38–39)

Covey explains how quickly his irritation evaporated and compassion took over, but he had to move out of his own experience to come to understand the father and his children's experience. Understanding made room for compassion and love. It is easy to see how Covey felt irritated without understanding the man's story, and it is also easy to see how small Covey may have felt after he understood the man had just lost his wife. Thich Nhat Hanh reminds us, "Love is understanding. If you cannot understand, you cannot love" (1991, p. 275).

The Buddha teaches the Four Noble Truths as the path to liberation from suffering. As explained by Jeffrey Rubin in his book, *Psychotherapy and Buddhism*, "This doctrine [the Four Noble Truths] delineates the symptom, diagnosis, prognosis, and treatment plan for addressing human suffering" (1996, p. 17). Kornfield teaches, "The Four Noble Truths insist that we face our pain, the pain in our body and mind and the pain of the world. They teach us to stop running away. Only by courageously opening to the sorrow of the world as it is can we find our freedom" (2008, p. 243). As with individuation, one must see one's pain as it is and the pain of the world. One cannot deny it, hide from it, or run away from it. The pain of the world is the collective shadow, and it must be given a voice, like one's personal shadow or unconscious.

The First Noble Truth states that existence will inevitably bring about pain. All of us will suffer from aging, sickness, and death. Rubin explains, "The first Noble Truth presents the salient characteristic of human life, *Duhkha*, a Sanskrit word for awryness, unsatisfactoriness, and suffering" (1996, p. 17). One will suffer; what she does with that suffering will determine her state of liberation or not. Kornfield explains, "Facing our pain and suffering honorably is the only way we can grow" (2008, p. 244). One must allow the grief, longing, fear, anger, and sadness to be felt in order to grow; we must walk through it. Jacquelyn's teacher and friend, Steve Allred, MFT has often said in conversation (2008), "The closer you walk to the center of your pain, the more healing you will find on the other side." Kornfield goes on to say, "There is a sacred quality to the witnessing of our suffering that is different from suppression or repression. This witnessing is an essential part of meditation, an attentive and compassionate awareness. Sometimes witnessing is all we have to do. At other times after witnessing, a strong response is necessary. Either way, our suffering must be borne consciously" (2008, p. 246). Meditation is a tool to bring forth that which has been repressed; as responses become conscious, one goes through pain to healing. The tightness around emotions begins to loosen and the letting go or the liberation begins.

The second Noble Truth describes the causes of suffering to be desire, attachment, and craving. Rubin explains, "There are three types of desire: desire for sense gratification, existence or nonexistence, and the clinging to self. . . . Suffering arises when we resist the flow of life and cling to things, events, people, and ideas as permanent" (1996, pp. 17–18). The more one tries to control others and situations, holding tightly to a specific outcome, the more she will suffer. The psychology of Buddhism teaches its student that control is an illusion which creates suffering. Kornfield points out, "The Second Noble Truth tells us that when we grasp, we create suffering. . . . Suffering is like rope burn. We need to let go" (2008, p. 247).

The third Noble Truth is the way to freedom—suffering can be eliminated. As explained by Rubin, "It is possible, according to Buddhism, to extricate oneself from psychological imprisonment and to reach a state of complete awakening or liberation called Nirvana, which means 'to blow out' or 'to extinguish.' What is extinguished is personal desire. In this state grasping and suffering have disappeared and the oneness of all life is evident" (1996, p. 18). When the desire to have a life different than what is has been extinguished, peace arises. This does not mean one does not strive for personal excellence and greatness. It is about the acceptance of what is present without hiding behind any facades or excuses.

The blessing is in the journey of becoming more whole, not the desire to change the outcome. The psychology of Buddhism does not teach its student to rid herself of desire. It teaches its student to differentiate between healthy and unhealthy desire, finding balance.

The Fourth Noble Truth is the path to end suffering, through the Noble Eightfold Path. As Ruben reads it:

> The Fourth Noble Truth provides the map of how to experience enlightenment: the Noble Eightfold Path, which comprises right understanding or accurate awareness into the reality of life; right thought or aspiration; right speech, speaking truthfully and compassionately; right action, abstaining from killing, lying, stealing, adultery, and misuse of intoxicants; right livelihood, engaging

in occupations that promote rather than harm life; right effort, or the balanced effort to be aware; right mindfulness, seeing things as they are, and right concentration or meditative attentiveness. (1996, p. 18)

The precepts which make up the Noble Eightfold Path are set up as guidelines and self-check points, creating more awareness and consciousness of one's present experience. There will always be deeper consciousness to uncover in one's mind; there will always be more awareness to attain unto. This was the Buddha's experience of being liberated from ignorance:

> Ignorance had been the jail keeper. . . . Clouded by endless waves of deluded thoughts, the mind had falsely divided reality into subject and object, self and others, existence and non-existence, birth and death, and from these discriminations arose wrong views—the prisons of feelings, craving, grasping, and becoming. The suffering of birth, old age, sickness, and death only made the prison walls thicker. The only thing to do was to seize the jailkeeper and see his true face. The jailkeeper was ignorance. And the means to overcome ignorance were the Noble Eightfold Path. Once the jailkeeper was gone, the jail would disappear and never be rebuilt again. (in Hanh, 1991, p. 121)

The jailkeeper does not regain position because the mind is constantly questioning that which is. This dispels ignorance. Thich Nhat Hanh goes on to say, "The Noble Eightfold Path is the path of living in awareness. Mindfulness is the foundation. By practicing mindfulness, you can develop concentration which enables you to attain understanding. . . . Mindfulness leads to concentration and understanding which liberates you from every pain and sorrow and leads to peace and joy" (1991, p. 147). Compassion is the result of accurate understanding. Compassion changes the world.

In order to feel empathy and compassion we must look deeply into our own psyche. To meet another person with compassion we must understand our own pain and make peace with the suffering in our own life. When we look into our own pain we honor it, it lives, it is not pushed down or disowned; only then can we honor another person's pain. Ladner explains,

> If we do not find a way of facing the difficult aspects of our own souls, a way of looking honestly at our suffering and its causes in order to develop a meaningful, mature compassion for ourselves, then regardless of what we do externally, a sense of emptiness or incompleteness will remain in our hearts. We will not become deeply compassionate toward others, and we will not find freedom from suffering in our own lives. (2004, p. 51)

The process of seeing through the illusion of one's ego, one's complexes and projections is not an easy task. It takes courage to challenge the fragility of the ego. Ladner explains, "If we fail to see through our projections and to develop even-mindedness, there is a real danger that we will allow the self-centered ego to be in control of our efforts to develop compassion" (2004, p. 117). If the self-centered ego is in control of one's effort to develop compassion, she will be acting from the ego's agenda which is never true compassion. She may be seeking praise and worthiness through her acts of service, thereby diluting her potency and effectiveness. It becomes a charade. Jack Kornfield expounds:

> If our actions will bring harm to others, even in the service of some "good," they are almost certainly deluded. If our actions do not come from a kind heart, from loving courage and compassion, they are deluded. If they are based on a distinction between "us" and "them," they stem from delusion. Only to the extent that we act from the wisdom of no separation, understanding how we are woven together, will our intention bring benefit. (2008, p. 264)

As the reader may recall, this is similar to when Jacquelyn first started in hospice care. She wanted to be the volunteer with deep compassion. Ego-based wanting to be deeply compassionate was the very thing that put her ego in charge, making her service about herself—not Mary.

As one makes the complexes, projections, and shadow parts conscious, she takes responsibility for her own life and that which is manifesting in all facets of her experience. There is no longer an option to blame that which is outside of herself for the challenges she faces. With responsibility comes the state of mind which seeks to connect with compassion to the rest of the world. When I am responsible for the state of my life, for the state of the world, I am no longer blaming those people over there or that other country. When I am not blaming the other for her struggles, I am able to see their struggles as well, knowing that their struggle does not diminish my own—both sides exist and are real. They exist side by side, neither minimizing the other. This is seeing how we are similar yet different.

Our struggles are what bring us commonality, from a state of wholeness one is able to move from an empathetic understanding to the action of compassion. We can only change ourselves, and when we do, we begin to interact with the world in more effective ways and the world seems to change with us. Jung describes the effects of such consciousness:

> If you imagine someone who is brave enough to withdraw these projections, all and sundry, then you get an individual conscious of a pretty thick shadow.... He

has become a serious problem to himself, as he is now unable to say that *they* do this or that, *they* are wrong and *they* must be fought against. . . . Such a man knows that whatever is wrong in the world is in himself, and if he only learns to deal with his own shadow then he has done something real for the world. He has succeeded in removing an infinitesimal part at least of the unsolved gigantic, social problems of our day. (1940/1969, pp. 101–102)

Being whole psychologically means one loves because one sees her partner more accurately. Both parties are less jaded by fears; both parties feel seen, heard, and understood, creating safety and trust. This is a relationship based in compassion and empathy. As explained in Ciaramicoli and Ketcham, "Empathy teaches us how to protect ourselves and others by striving to avoid deception in everything we say and do. This can be a hard road, requiring commitment, willpower, discipline, patience, and endurance. Yet only through the power of empathy can we discover who we really are, who we are meant to become, and how we can help others in their search to find themselves" (2000, p. 148). As more personalities become whole, more interpersonal relationships will reflect these values, creating a world with more kindness, more connection, more authenticity, more joy, and more peace.

Psychological wholeness creates space for differing opinions and experiences, without being threatening. A mind that lives with wholeness experiences life with less fear, anxiety, and defensiveness. She is curious about the world. She knows that she is enough. She is not addicted to performance or praise, striving for personal excellence rather than to become better than others. Psychological wholeness shows kind self-talk; it does not call oneself stupid or useless. One who is psychologically whole understands she is human and honors her limitations not as a deficit but as a part of the whole of her being. Psychological wholeness does not seek to control others through manipulation or by creating fearful and unsafe environments. A person who lives in psychological wholeness is not possessed by the need to be the center of attention all the time, or the most important part of the team—there is room for everyone to have their moment to shine. A person with psychological wholeness is excited for others' successes and champions others on their journey because the success of others does not reflect a lack in oneself; it is a victory for human greatness. A psychologically whole person seeks self-knowledge and the experience of unity.

The lessons of unity, compassion, and empathy taught through the psychology of Buddhism are learned and understood at a deeper level when individuation is a part of the foundation. The individuation process helps the seeker to see past her complexes, projections, and balance her shadow with curiosity. Buddhism propels these processes forward in time with further self-awareness through meditation and (deceptively) simple precepts that encourage freedom from toxic thinking patterns and a deep understanding of the oneness that connects us all. Thich Nhat Hanh explains, "With mindfulness—the practice of peace—we can begin by working to transform the wars in ourselves" (2007, p. 92). Kornfield concludes, "There is no separation between inner and outer, self and other. Tending ourselves, we tend the world. Tending the world, we tend ourselves" (2008, p. 356). It is the inner which transforms the outer.

Ladner supports the idea that "we must become peaceful ourselves if we wish to create a world in which long-term peace is possible" (2004, p. 234). As more hearts begin to cherish understanding we will create a world which embraces compassion. As more human beings find peace within, we will find ourselves a part of a more peaceful world.

Through correct understanding one gains the aptitude to act with compassion for oneself and others who are seen as brothers and sisters. At this point she has become a personality who may evoke powerful change in the world. A Jewish tale makes this point touchingly:

> An old Hasidic rabbi asked his pupils how they could tell when the night had ended and day begun, for daybreak is the time for certain holy prayers. "Is it," proposed one student, "when you can see an animal in the distance and tell whether it is a sheep or a dog?" "No," answered the rabbi. "Is it when you can clearly see the lines on your own palm?" "Is it when you can look at a tree in the distance and tell if it is a fig or a pear tree?" "No," answered the rabbi each time. "Then what is it?" the pupils demanded. "It is when you can look on the face of any man or woman and see that they are your sister or brother. Until then it is still night. (Kornfield, 2008, p. 390)

The day the light dawns on our planet is the day the earth breathes a sigh of relief as she sees her children working together to tend each other with love and respect as well as honor her wellness as a planet.

The psychology of Buddhism coupled with the individuation process of depth psychology guides us effectively to the center of one's self. Through the pain and anguish of dismantling the ego and its protective facades, she emerges, as the phoenix rising from the ashes, a human being with enough clarity to comprehend and value the unity of all that lives.

Conclusion

The Limits of War and Peace in Education and Therapy

"Blessed are the peacemakers, for they shall be called the children of God."

(Matthew 5:9)

We hope that it has been clear from the outset of this study that we have not written it because we are bold enough to believe that if only everyone followed the ideas we have laid out here, humankind would soon be free from war. That would be both unforgivably presumptuous and colossally naïve. War, which derives from ideological, political, and territorial conflicts, has always been a fact of human existence. Its complete elimination, if it be possible at all, lies in a future that we will not live to see, nor will our children, nor even, probably, our grandchildren.

What we *have* proposed, drawing from our fields of expertise, education and psychology, is that there are theoretical models and practical modalities available to us to make peaceful resolution of conflicts more possible and the resort to war less likely *now* and, increasingly, in the future. What we have proposed is a beginning of principled and concerted efforts in schools and consulting rooms—education and therapy interlinked in both theory and practice—to make us ever more disposed to peaceful resolution of conflict and ever less likely to resort to shots fired in anger. Ours is a "gradualist" approach. We offer no panaceas—just the best in scholarship and practice that we have been able to assemble in order to work, step-by-step, toward the idea of a more peaceful planet.

And even if war is avoidable, conflict is not. Nor should it be. It is woven into the dialectical nature of things. For it is a universal principle that opposition is the *sine qua non* of progression. It is opposition that calls out for the remedy to the strife that progression beyond it requires. Rather, peaceful forward movement occurs when polar opposites meld into a new, third position that includes at least some of the elements of each of the opposites resulting in a workable way forward along the lines of that third position. This third position ultimately transcends both of the formerly antipathetic poles. We are not calling for an elimination of opposition, for opposition is an ontological and even psychological necessity for growth to occur. Rather, we are calling for gentler and more generative ways to resolve conflict.

However, as Einstein said, a problem cannot be solved at the level at which it was created. Rather, our inquiries and actions must move up a level—epistemologically, ontologically, ethically—for a solution to even be able to be envisaged in a third, higher perspective and approach. But therein lies the rub, for "Tertium non datur": "The third is not given," as the Latin maxim goes. We must work to imagine it and then work to bring it into existence. Jung called this in psychological terms "the transcendent function."

This study has aimed to be a part—however modest—of that work which is necessary to effect those changes in individuals and cultures; changes, we hope, that will move us forward and upward in our theoretical discourses and practical agendas toward the ideal of a world free from war and its incalculable horrors. And although such a paradisiacal state of affairs can probably only be fully realized by the direct intervention of Deity in our individual and collective lives, this does not absolve us of the duty to lend this cause our best efforts. Indeed, it defines that duty. For, as President Kennedy said in his inaugural address, "Here on earth, God's work must truly be our own." This book represents one such effort to make God's work our own.

We have tried to avoid an approach to human interaction that is so sanguine about the prospects for peace that it simply strikes the reader as too wild eyed and optimistic to lend much credence to. On the other hand, we have wanted to avoid the opposite error of "quietism"—or being so resigned to the evils that abound in the world that one simply gives up on any attempt to remediate them. Ours is that middle way wherein one prays, in the much-beloved words of the great twentieth-century, Protestant-existentialist theologian Reinhold Niebuhr: "God, grant me the serenity to accept the things I cannot change, the courage to change the things I can, and the wisdom to know the difference."

Accordingly, in the service of reason and fair-mindedness, we began with a quick survey of some of the leading opposing voices in twentieth-century depth psychology—our area of inquiry and action—of those who argued not only that war would always be with us but that there seemed to be virtually no prospect of changing that situation to any significant degree. We attended to the lachrymose wisdom of various philosophers and military theorists who sadly concluded that war might even become more widespread and more terrible in its consequences because of the new technologies of the twenty-first century that would lead to an increase in both the frequency and intensity of warfare. Not only that, but some have argued that war serves various important spiritual, emotional, and, of course, political needs that human beings would not renounce even if they could.

We paid close attention to these great thinkers and writers and their theories about war, which rested on the conviction that nothing could or would change in human history regarding warfare except its possible escalation. Nevertheless, we found others whose thoughts and statements were more compelling, more moving, and more likely to inspire us and others to engage in processes of interpersonal and intrapersonal transformations that would take us off the warpath. In other words, we looked finally to those whose purpose has been to help us catch the vision of a vastly more enlightened, less violent world. The Dalai Lama, Thich Nhat Hanh, Dr. Martin Luther King, and Mahatma Gandhi have envisioned it, conveyed that vision, and, in some cases, died for that vision. This study represents the authors' efforts to help ensure that these people did not live and die in vain in and for that vision.

As for those interpersonal and intrapersonal theoretical structures and daily, worldly practices that might promote both inner and outer growth in the quest for peace, we looked primarily at the classroom in education and the consulting room in psychology as two primary sites where these inner- and intrapersonal metamorphoses could be carried on and carried out in an appropriate, credible, and durable way.

In psychotherapy, we examined the possibilities of Buddhist psychology and its dedication to inner-focused peace and outer-directed compassion most useful in promoting the bloodless resolution of conflict. C. G. Jung's archetypal psychology—also known as analytical psychology—was equally important in showing us the necessity of withdrawing and owning one's own shadow in the service of the sane resolution of conflict. This entails not projecting one's own shadow upon others, which is an ineffective, immature way of dealing with the evil that lies inside each of us and that, when projected onto others, demonizes them and makes us inclined to take up arms against them. Here, said Jung, is the true root cause of war. Thus, if we would create peace in the world, we must first discover it in ourselves.

Psychologically, this means engaging in processes of attaining to, or at least working toward, individuation and enlightenment. In education, it means promoting practices that lead the student to a more vibrant and hopeful construction of his life-narrative. It encourages the student to accomplish, by means of the material in the curriculum, a synthesis of his many aspects, tendencies, and commitments into an "integral" personality. It aims at his adoption of a more empathic view of ideas and their manifestation in cultural forms that are not like those of his own culture.

These things point to the desirability of what Mayes has called "education for individuation" and a holistic multicultural pedagogy in the classroom (whether the classroom is actual or virtual) as well as psychotherapeutic practices in the consulting room that attend closely to the precepts and practice of Buddhist meditation and that courageously take up the Jungian challenge to individuate as an existential imperative both psychically and ethically. They also point to the crucial importance of a pedagogically balanced and holistic (not a politically excessive and polemical) multiculturalism of mutual edification in which each student learns from all and all students learn from each.

For this to happen, Buber's pedagogical ethic of I-Thou dialogical partnering must be the prevailing discursive ethos and practice in the classroom, not the mind-numbing, soul-destroying I-It *non*-communications of standardized education, for this turns the teacher and student alike into mere objects—a state of affairs that can only ultimately lead to anger, depression, acting out, and a sense of self-betrayal. What is more, it breeds political economies that, Right or Left, alternately terrorize or seduce the individual into the political and ethical quicksand of inauthenticity and alienation in a Total State that robs him and others of their dignity as human beings and as children of the Divine.

Indeed, it is in this ennobling vision of the potential divinity of the individual that this study is rooted and toward which it has aimed. It is a vision that turns entirely upon the ideas of passion and compassion—passion for a more creative, generative, and just world peopled by individuals who discover the divine in themselves by discovering it in others and the divine in others by discovering it in themselves. With them, we join the great Ulysses in Lord Tennyson's poem in declaring, even in the midst of the plague-winds of war: "Come, my friends, 'tis not too late to seek a newer world."

Bibliography

Adler, A. (1966). The psychology of power. *Journal of Individual Psychology, 22*(2), 166–172.

Aichhorn, A. (1935/1965). *Wayward youth: A psychoanalytic study of delinquent children, illustrated by actual case histories.* New York: Viking Press.

Anderson, C. A., & Dill, K. E. (2000). Video games and aggressive thoughts, feelings, and behavior in the laboratory and in life. *Journal of Personality and Social Psychology, 78,* 772–790.

Anderson, C. A., Shibuya, S., Ihori, N., Swing, E. L., Bushman, B. J., Sakamoto, A., Rothstein, H. R., & Saleem, M. (2010). Violent video game effects on aggression, empathy, and prosocial behavior in eastern and western countries: A meta-analytic review. *Psychological Bulletin, 136*(2), 151–173.

Anderson, N. B., Belar, C. D., Breckler, S. J., Nordal, K. C., Ballard, D. W., Bufka, L. F., Bossolo, L., Bethune, S., Brownawell, A., & Wiggins, K. (2015, February 4). *Stress in America: Paying with our health.* American Psychological Association. https://www.apa.org/news/press/releases/stress/2014/stress-report.pdf

Armstrong, K. (2010). *Twelve steps to a compassionate life.* Random House.

Assagioli, R. (1965). *Psychosynthesis: A manual of principles and techniques.* Penguin Group.

Austin, J. H. (1999). *Zen and the brain.* The MIT Press.

Barasch, M. I. (2009). *The compassionate life.* Berrett-Koehler Publishers.

Berliner, D., & Biddle, B. (1995). *The manufactured crisis: Myths, fraud, and the attack upon America's public schools.* Reading, MA: Addison Wesley.

Black, J. (1998). *Why wars happen.* Reaktion Books.

Blair, H. T., Schafe, G. E., Bauer, E. P., Rodrigues, S. M., & LeDoux, J. E. (2001). Synaptic plasticity in the lateral amygdala: A cellular hypothesis of fear conditioning. *Learning & Memory, 8,* 229–242. http://www.learnmem.org/cgi/doi/10.1101/lm.30901

Blumer, H. (1969). *Symbolic interactionism.* Prentice-Hall.

Bordo, S. (1987). *The flight of objectivity: Essays on Cartesianism and culture.* SUNYP.

Brown, G., Phillips, M., & Shapiro, S. (1976). *Getting it all together: Confluent education.* Phi Delta Kappa Educational Foundation.

Brown, M. (1981). *Laying waste: The poisoning of America by toxic chemicals.* Washington Square Press.

Buber, M. (1965). *I and thou.* Vintage.

Buber, M. (1985). *Between man and man.* Scribners.

Bullough, R. V., Jr., Patterson, R. S., & Mayes, C. (2002). Teaching as prophecy. *Curriculum Inquiry, 32*(3), 341–348.

Campbell, J. (2007). *The mythic dimension.* New World Library.

Carey, N. (2012). *The epigenetics revolution: How modern biology is rewriting our understanding of genetic disease and inheritance.* Columbia University Press.

Castoriadis, C. (1994). Psychoanalysis and politics. In S. Shamdasani and M. Münchow (Eds.), *Speculations after Freud: Psychoanalysis, philosophy, and culture* (pp. 1–12). London: Routledge.

Ciaramicoli, A. P., & Ketcham, K. (2000). *The power of empathy.* Penguin Group.

Chodron, P. (2006). *Practicing peace in times of war.* Shambhala Publications.

Covey, S. R. (2004). *The 7 habits of highly effective people.* Simon & Schuster. (Original work published 1989)

Crain, W. (2010). *Theories of development: Concepts and applications.* Prentice-Hall.

Cremin, L. (1964). *The transformation of the school: Progressivism in American education, 1876–1957.* Vintage Press.

Cremin, L. (1988). *American education: The metropolitan experience.* Harper and Row.

Dalai Lama. (2011). *Beyond religion: Ethics for a whole world.* Houghton Mifflin Harcourt Publishing.

Davidson, R. J., & Begley, S. (2012). *The emotional life of your brain.* Penguin Group.

Davidson, R. J., Dunne, J., Eccles, J. S., Engle, A., Greenberg, M., Jennings, P., Jha, A., Jinpa, T., Lantieri, L., Meyer, D., Roeser, R. W., & Vago, D. (2012). Contemplative practices and mental training: Prospects for American education. *Child Development Perspectives, 6*(2), 146–153. https://doi.org/10.1111/j.1750-8606.2012.00240.x

Davidson, R. J., & Harrington, A. (Eds.). (2002). *Visions of compassion.* Oxford University Press.

Deikman, A. (1982). *The observing self: Mysticism and psychotherapy.* Beacon Press.

Devine, D. (1996). Prejudice and out-group perception. In A. Tesser (Ed.), *Advanced social psychology* (pp. 467–524). McGraw-Hill.

Dewey, J. (1916). *Democracy and education.* Macmillan.

Dispenza, J. (2014). *You are the placebo: Making your mind matter.* Hay House.

Ehrenreich, B. (2011). *Blood rites: Origins and history of the passions of war.* Granta Books. (Original work published 1997)

Eliade, M. (1974). *Shamanism: Archaic techniques of ecstasy.* Princeton University Press.

Eliot, T. S. (1971). *T.S. Eliot: The complete poems and plays: 1909–1950.* Harcourt, Brace and World.

Ellenberger, H. (1970). *The discovery of the unconscious: The history and evolution of dynamic psychiatry.* Basic Books.

Epstein, M. (2007). *Psychotherapy without the self: A Buddhist perspective.* Yale University Press.

Fay, B. (1987). *Critical Social Science: Liberation and its limits.* Cornell University Press.

Fay, B. (2000). *Contemporary philosophy of social science: A multicultural approach.* Blackwell Publishers.

Ferrer, J. (2002). *Revisioning transpersonal theory: A participatory vision of human spirituality.* Albany: State University of New York Press.

Ferrucci, P. (1982). *What we may be: Techniques for psychological and spiritual growth through psychosynthesis.* Jeremy Tarcher.

Fields, D. R. (2010). Neuroscience. Change in the brain's white matter. *Science, 330*(6005), 768–769. https://doi.org/10.1126/science.1199139

Forbes, S. (2003). *Holistic education: An analysis of its nature and ideas.* Foundation for Educational Renewal Press.

Fornari, F. (1975). *The psychoanalysis of war.* (Translated by A. Pfeifer). Doubleday & Company. (Original work published 1966)

Fraga, M. F., Ballestar, E., Paz, M. F., Ropero, S., Setien, F., Ballestar, M. L., Heine-Suñer, D., Cigudosa, J. C., Urioste, M., Benitez, J., Boix-Chornet, M., Sanchez-Aguilera, A., Ling, C., Carlsson, E., Poulsen, P., Vaag, A., Stephan, Z., Spector, T. D., Wu, Y. Z., Plass, C., ... Esteller, M. (2005). Epigenetic differences arise during the lifetime of monozygotic twins. *Proceedings of the National Academy of Sciences of the United States of America, 102*(30), 10604–10609. https://doi.org/10.1073/pnas.0500398102

Freud, A. (1930). *Introduction to psychoanalysis: Lectures for child analysts and teachers, 1922–1935.* International Universities Press.

Freud, S. (1957/1923). The ego and the id. In J. Rickman (Ed.), *A general selection from the works of Sigmund Freud* (pp. 210–235). Doubleday Anchor Books.

Freud, S. (1981). Why war? In J. Strachey (Ed. & Trans.), *The standard edition of the complete psychological works of Sigmund Freud* (Vol. 22, pp. 197–215). The Hogarth Press. (Original work published 1964)

Gadamer, H. (1980). *Dialogue and dialectic: Eight hermeneutical studies on Plato.* Yale University Press.

Garfinkel, H. (1967). *Studies in ethnomethodology.* Englewood Cliffs, NJ: Prentice Hall.

Gellert, M. (2001). *The fate of America: An inquiry into national character.* Washington, DC: Brassey's.

Giddens, A. (1991). *Modernity and self-identity: Self and society in the late modern age.* Stanford: Stanford University Press.

Gitlin, T. (1995). *The twilight of common dreams: Why America is wracked by culture wars.* New York: Holt.

Goleman, D. (1995). *Emotional intelligence: Why it can matter more than IQ.* Bantam Books.

Gray, R. (1996). *Archetypal explorations: An integrative approach to human behavior.* London: Routledge.

Greene, M. (1974). Cognition, consciousness, and curriculum. In W. Pinar (Ed.), *Heightened consciousness, cultural revolution, and curriculum theory* (pp. 69–83). McCutchan Publishing.

Grossman, D. (2009). *On killing: The psychological cost of learning to kill in war and society.* Back Bay Books.

Grossman, D., & DeGaetano, G. (1999) *Stop teaching our kids to kill: A call to action against tv, movie, and video game violence.* Crown Publishers.

Guenther, H., & Kawamura, L. (2005). *Mind in Buddhist psychology.* Dharma Press.

Hall, G. S. (1904). *Adolescence: Its psychology and its relations to physiology, anthropology, sociology, sex, crime, religion and education.* D. Appleton and Company.

Hanh, T. N. (1991). *Old path white clouds.* Parallax Press.

Hanh, T. N. (2001). *Anger: Wisdom for cooling the flames.* River Head Books.

Hanh, T. N. (2007). *Living Buddha, living Christ.* Penguin Group.

Hatch, O. G., & Senate Committee on the Judiciary (1999). *Children, violence, and the media: A report for parents and policy makers.*

Heath, S. (1983). *Ways with words: Language, life, and work in communities and classrooms.* Cambridge University Press.

Hedges, C. (2003). *War is a force that gives us meaning.* First Anchor Books. (Original work published 2002).

Herrigel, E. (1971). *Zen and the art of archery.* Vintage Book.

Hilgard, E. (1987). *Psychology in America: A historical survey.* Harcourt Brace Jovanovich.

Hillman, J. (2005). *A terrible love of war.* The Penguin Group.

Hirschfelder, A., & Molin, P. (1992). *The encyclopedia of Native American religions: A comprehensive guide to the traditions and practices of North American Indians.* MJF Books.

Homans, P. (1999). *The ability to mourn: Disillusionment and the social origins of psychoanalysis.* University of Chicago Press.

Huebner, D. (1999). *The lure of the transcendent: Collected essays by Dwayne E. Huebner.* Lawrence Erlbaum Associates.

Ignatieff, M. (1985). *The needs of strangers.* Viking Penguin.

Isaacs, S. (1932). *The children we teach, seven to eleven years.* University of London Press.

James, W. (1916). *A pluralistic universe.* Longmans, Green, and Co.

Jansz, J., & van Drunen, P. (2004). *A social history of psychology.* Blackwell Publishing Ltd.

Jung, C. G. (1953). *Two essays on analytical psychology* (Volume 7 in the *Collected Works*). (R. F. C. Hull, Trans.). Princeton University Press.

Jung, C. G. (1966). *The practice of psychotherapy, Collected works of C. G. Jung, Vol 16*. Translated by Gerhard Adler and R.F.C. Hull. Princeton University Press.

Jung, C. G. (1969). Psychology and religion. In H. Read et al. (Eds.), *The collected works of C. G. Jung: Vol. 11. Psychology and religion* (2nd ed., pp. 3–105). Princeton University Press. (Original work published 1940). https://doi.org/10.1515/9781400850983.3

Jung, C. G. (1969). A review of the complex theory (R. F. C. Hull, Trans.). In H. Read et al. (Eds.), *The collected works of C. G. Jung: Vol. 8. Structure and dynamics of the psyche* (2nd ed., pp. 92–104). Princeton University Press. (Original work published 1948). https://doi.org/10.1515/9781400850952.92

Jung, C. G. (1968). *The collected works of C. G. Jung: Vol. 9 pt. 2. Aion: Researches into the phenomenology of the self* (R. F. C. Hull, Trans.) (H. Read et al., Eds.). Princeton University Press. (Original work published 1951). https://doi.org/10.1515/9781400851058

Jung, C. G. (1970a). *The collected works of C. G. Jung: Vol. 14. Mysterium coniunctionis* (R. F. C. Hull, Trans.) (H. Read et al., Eds.). Princeton University Press. (Original work published 1955–1956) https://doi.org/10.1515/9781400850853

Jung, C. G. (1970b). The undiscovered self (present and future) (R. F. C. Hull, Trans). In H. Read et al. (Eds.), *The collected works of C. G. Jung: Vol. 10. Civilization in transition* (2nd ed., pp. 247–305). Princeton University Press. (Original work published 1957). https://doi.org/10.1515/9781400850976.247

Jung, C. G. (1970c). Flying saucers: A modern myth of things seen in the skies (R. F. C. Hull, Trans.). In H. Read et al. (Eds.), *The collected works of C. G. Jung: Vol. 10. Civilization in transition* (2nd ed., pp. 307–433). Princeton University Press. (Original work published 1958). https://doi.org/10.1515/9781400850976.307

Jung, C. G. (1983). *The essential Jung*. Edited by A. Storr. Princeton University Press.

Kessler, R. C., Berglund, P. A., Bruce, M. L., Koch, J. R., Laska, E. M., Leaf, P. J., Manderscheid, R. W., Rosenheck, R. A., Walters, E. E., & Wang, P. S. (2001). The prevalence and correlates of untreated serious mental illness. *Health Services Research, 36*(6), 987–1007.

Kessler, R. C., McGonagle, K. A., Zhao, S., Nelson, C. B., Hughes, M., Eshleman, S., Wittchen, H., & Kendler, K. (1994). Lifetime and 12-month prevalence of DSM-III-R Psychiatric Disorders in the United States: Results from the national comorbidity survey. *Archives of General Psychiatry, 51*, 8–19.

Kierkegaard, S. (1969). *A Kierkegaard anthology*. Edited by R. Bretall. Princeton University Press.

King, M. L., Jr. (1992). *I have a dream: Writings & speeches that changed the world*. Edited by J. M. Washington. HarperCollins Publishers. (Original work published 1986)

Kohlberg, L. (1987). *Child psychology and childhood education: A cognitive-developmental view*. New York: Longman.

Kornfield, J. (1993). *A path with heart*. Bantam Dell.

Kornfield, J. (2008). *The wise heart*. Bantam Dell.

Kozol, J. (1991). *Savage inequalities: Children in American schools.* Harper.
Ladner, L. (2004). *The lost art of compassion.* HarperCollins Publishers.
Lasch, C. (1991). *The culture of narcissism.* Norton & Company. (Original work published 1979)
LeShan, L. (2002). *The psychology of war: Comprehending its mystique and its madness.* Helios Press. (Original work published 1992)
Lynch, K. (2013, October 8). Confirmed: Grand theft auto 5 breaks 6 sales world records. Guinness World Records. https://www.guinnessworldrecords.com/news/2013/10/confirmed-grand-theft-auto-breaks-six-sales-world-records-51900/
Maslow, A. (1968). *Toward a psychology of being* (2nd ed.). D. Van Nostrand.
Mattoon, M. (1985). *Jungian psychology in perspective.* New York: The Free Press.
Mayes, C. (2002). The teacher as an archetype of spirit. *Journal of Curriculum Studies, 34*(6), 699–718.
Mayes, C. (2003). *Teaching mysteries: Foundations of a spiritual pedagogy.* University Press of America.
Mayes, C. (2005). *Jung and education: Elements of an archetypal pedagogy.* Rowman & Littlefield Education Press.
Mayes, C., & Ferrin, S. (2001). Spiritually committed public-school teachers. Their beliefs of spiritually committed public school teachers concerning religious expression in the classroom. *Religion and Education, 28*(1), 75–94.
Mayes, C., Maile Cutri, R., Goslin, N., & Montero, F. (2016). *Understanding the whole student: Holistic multicultural education* (2nd ed). Rowman & Littlefield.
Mayo Clinic. (2021, March 24). Stress symptoms: Effects on your body and behavior. https://www.mayoclinic.org/healthy-lifestyle/stress-management/in-depth/stress-symptoms/art-20050987
Miller, J. (1988). *The holistic curriculum.* Toronto: The Ontario Institute for Studies in Education.
Miller, J. (2004). *The transcendent function: Jung's model of psychological growth through dialogue with the unconscious.* State University of New York Press.
Miller, R. (1990). *What are schools for? Holistic education in American culture.* Holistic Education Press.
Miller, J., & Seller, W. (1985). *Curriculum: perspectives and practices.* Longman.
Moffett, J. (1994). *The universal schoolhouse: Spiritual awakening through education.* Jossey-Bass Publishers.
Montagu, A. (1967). *The anatomy of swearing.* University of Pennsylvania Press.
Muscari, M. (2002). Media violence: advice for parents. *Pediatric Nursing, 28*(6), 585–591.
Nelson, P. (2000). Mystical experience and radical deconstruction: Through the ontological looking glass. In T. Hart, P. Nelson, and K. Puhakka (Eds.), *Transpersonal knowing: Exploring the horizon of consciousness* (pp. 55–84). State University of New York Press.
Noddings, N. (1995). Care and moral education. In W. Kohli (Ed.), *Critical conversations in the philosophy of education* (pp. 137–148). Longman.

Odajnyk, V. (1976). *Jung and politics: The political and social ideas of C. G. Jung*. Harper and Row.
Oschman, J. L. (2006). Trauma energetics. *Journal of Bodywork and Movement Therapies, 10*, 21–34. https://doi.org/10.1016/j.jbmt.2005.10.001
Pfister, O. (1922). *Psycho-analysis in the service of education, being an introduction to psycho-analysis*. Henry Kimpton.
Phenix, P. (1964). *Realms of meaning: A philosophy of curriculum for general education*. McGraw Hill.
Piaget, J., & Inhelder, B. (1969). *The psychology of the child*. Basic Books.
Pinker, S. (2011). *The better angels of our nature: Why violence has declined*. Penguin Group.
Potter, J. W. (1999). *On media violence*. Sage Publications.
Preece, R. (2006). *The wisdom of imperfection—The challenge of individuation in Buddhist life*. Snow Lion Publications.
Progoff, I. (1959). *Depth psychology and modern man: A new view of the magnitude of human personality, its dimensions and resources*. New York: Julian Press.
Redl, F., & Wattenberg, W. (1951). *Mental hygiene in teaching*. Harcourt, Brace and Company.
Reinsmith, W. (1992). *Archetypal forms in teaching: A continuum*. Greenwood Press.
Rieff, P. (1987). *The triumph of the therapeutic: Uses of faith after Freud*. University of Chicago Press.
Rubin, J. B. (1996). *Psychotherapy and Buddhism: Towards an integration*. Plenum Press.
Salzberger-Wittenberg, I. (1989). *The emotional experience of learning and teaching*. Routledge and Kegan Paul.
Schipani, D. (1988). *Religious education encounters liberation theology*. Religious Education Press.
Schutz, W. (1976). Education and the body. In G. Hendricks and J. Fadiman (Eds.), *Transpersonal education: A curriculum for feeling and being* (pp. 104–110). Prentice-Hall.
Scotton, B., Chinen, A., & Battista, J. (Eds.). (1996). *Textbook of transpersonal psychiatry and psychology*. Basic Books.
Siegel, D. J. (2007). *The mindful brain: Reflections and attunement in the cultivation of well-being*. Norton and Company.
Siegel, D. J. (2010). *Mindsight: The new science of personal transformation*. Random House Publishing.
Skinner, B. F. (1956). *The technology of teaching*. Appleton-Century-Croft.
Smith, H. (1958). *The religions of man*. Harper and Row, Publishers.
Spring, J. (1980). *Educating the worker-citizen*. McGraw Hill.
Stevens, A. (1995). Jungian approach to human aggression with special emphasis on war. *Agressive Behavior, 21*(1), 3–11. https://doi.org/10.1002/1098-2337(1995)21:1<3::AID-AB2480210103>3.0.CO;2-V
Thurman, R. A. F. (2005). *Anger: The seven deadly sins*. Oxford University Press.

Tillich, P. (1959). *Theology of culture*. Oxford University Press.
Tillich, P. (1976). *The shaking of the foundations*. Scribners.
Tremmel, R. (1993). Zen and the art of reflective practice in teacher education. *Harvard Educational Journal, 63*(4), 434–458.
Trostli, R. (1991). Educating as an art: The Waldorf approach. In R. Miller (Ed.), *New directions in education: Selections from Holistic Education Review* (p. 345). Holistic Education Press.
Twain, M. (1951). *The war prayer*. Harper & Row.
Vaughan, F. (1985). *The inward arc: Healing and wholeness in psychotherapy and spirituality*. New Science Library.
Von Franz, M. L. (1980). *Projection and re-collection in Jungian psychology: Reflections of the soul* (W. H. Kennedy, Trans.). Open Court Publishing (Original work published 1978).
Wacks, V., Jr. (1987). A case for self-transcendence as a purpose of adult education. *Adult Education Quarterly, 38*(1), 46–55.
Walsh, R., & Vaughan, F. (1993). Meditation: The royal road to the transpersonal. In R. Walsh and F. Vaughan (Eds.), *Paths beyond ego: The transpersonal vision* (pp. 47–55). Jeremy P. Tarcher.
Wheelwright, P. (1959). *Heraclitus*. Princeton University Press.
Whitmore, D. (1986). *Psychosynthesis in education: A guide to the joy of learning*. Destiny Books.
Wilber, K. (2000). *Integral psychology*. Shambhala.
Wiseman, T. (1996). A concept analysis of empathy. *Journal of Advanced Nursing, 23*, 1162–1167. http://doi.10.1046/j.1365-2648.1996.12213.x
Zachry, C. (1929). *Personality adjustments of school children, with an introduction by William Heard Kilpatrick*. C. Scribner's Sons.
Zinn, H. (1990). *A people's history of the United States*. Harper Perennial.

Index

Adler, A., x, xiv, 1, 4, 8, 11
anger, 13–15

Bodhisattva, the, 45–47
Buber, M., 71–73; dialogical partners, 26–27; *I and Thou*, 26; on Jesus as a teacher, 72
Buddhist psychology, 91–94

compassion: defined, ix–x, xvi–xvii, 40–41
complexes, 84–85

Dalai Lama, the, xviii, xxii, 19, 48–49
decentering, as educational goal, 23–24
depth psychology, 12–15; in the U.S. classroom (1922–2002), 5–7, 12–15
developmental theory, 23–25
Dewey, J., 6, 28, 33
dialectical spirituality, 64–67

education: as dehumanization and narcissism, 21–26; as decentering, 24; emotions in, 9–10; as repentance, 73–76; for individuation, 106

educative acts, 23–26
ego, the, 86
Einstein, A.: his letter to Freud, x–xi
emotion, as part of educational processes, 9–10
empathy, 42–43
epigenetics, 54–59

faith, religious, 70
Four Noble Truths, the, 96–97
Freire, P., 31, 36; *concientización*, 31–32

Gandhi, Mahatma, xviii, 105
Gradualist, approach to achieving peace, 104
Greene, M., 33; cubist curriculum, the, 20; pedagogy of care, 32

Hall, G. Stanley, 12; *Adolescence*, 12
Hanh, Thich Nhat, 93
Heath, Shirley Bryce, 21; students as "ethnographic detectives," 21
Hillman, J., x, xx–xxi
holistic education, 26–28, 37; requires confrontation with the shadow, 39

individual, the: as site of real change socially, 62–64
individuation, xiv–xvi, xx–xxi, 83–84

Jesus, as teacher, 72

Kierkegaard, S., 67–71
King, Martin Luther, Jr., xviii–xxi, 18
Kornfield, J., xi, xiii, xvi, 41, 44, 48, 92, 93, 94, 96, 97, 99, 101

law, limited uses of in promoting peace, 1–3

mass psychology, 62–63
Mayes, C., 14–25; *Understanding the Whole Student*, 37–39
meditation, 50–56; physiology of, 50–56; as prime instrument of peace, 60–62
military-industrial-educational complex, 32–33, 65–67
Miller, R., 27
Montague, A., 18–19

Noble Eightfold Path, the, 97–98
Noddings, N.: Pedagogy of Care, 33

Perennial Philosophy, the, 66
Pfister, O., 12
Progressivism, 12
projection, 17–18, 88–90

role transitivity, in teachers and students, 25–26

Self, the, xii
self-esteem, its role in cultivating compassion, 8
shadow, the, 15, 84–87
Steiner, R., 26–27

teaching, as a "religious" act, 73
transcendent function, the, 5–7; educational uses of, 5–7, 20
Transpersonal Theory, 65–67
Twain, M., 15–16

unconscious, the: engaging it as precondition of peace, 84–86
unitive spirituality, 64; in education, 65–67
unus mundus, the, xii–xiv

video games, as promoting violence, 28–31
violence, 60; as a result of trauma in one's life, 60–61; teaching, 16–17. *See also* video games
von Franz, M. L., xii, 17

Waldorf Schools, 26–28
war: archetypes of, 10; demystifying of, 28–30; root causes of, 4–5
wholeness, 101; the role of schools in promoting, 79–84

Zachry, C., 13; *Personality Adjustments of Schoolchildren* (1929), 13

www.ingramcontent.com/pod-product-compliance
Lightning Source LLC
Chambersburg PA
CBHW032216230426
43672CB00011B/2574